THE METHO

The first principle of *T...*
is that you will *never* ...
things you fear. Instead, ...
you into a regimen of diet, exercise, anti-stress
techniques, and step-by-step emergency procedures to
help you deal with your dreaded attacks. Most of all,
it will give your mind and body time to heal while
you are learning how to lessen the severity and frequency of attacks. Slowly and surely you will feel
stronger, calmer, more adequate, and able to face feared
situations with confidence.

THE PANIC ATTACK
RECOVERY BOOK

SHIRLEY ANNA SWEDE is the founder of
P.A.S.S. (Panic Attack Sufferers' Support Group).

SEYMOUR SHEPPARD JAFFE, M.D., is the
Chief Consultant for P.A.S.S. and Clinical Member
of the American Academy of Behavioral Medicine.

THE
PANIC ATTACK
RECOVERY BOOK

Shirley Swede
and
Seymour Sheppard Jaffe, M.D.

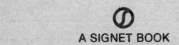

A SIGNET BOOK

NEW AMERICAN LIBRARY

A DIVISION OF PENGUIN BOOKS USA INC.

To Dr. Claire Weekes
for taking that first courageous step

NAL BOOKS ARE AVAILABLE AT QUANTITY DISCOUNTS
WHEN USED TO PROMOTE PRODUCTS OR SERVICES.
FOR INFORMATION PLEASE WRITE TO PREMIUM MARKETING DIVISION,
NEW AMERICAN LIBRARY, 1633 BROADWAY, NEW YORK, NEW YORK 10019.

NOTE TO THE READER
The ideas, procedures, and suggestions contained in this book are not intended as a substitute for consulting with your physician. All matters regarding your health require medical supervision.

The Panic Attack Recovery Book previously appeared in a Plume trade paperback edition published by New American Library.

SIGNET TRADEMARK REG. U.S. PAT. OFF. AND FOREIGN COUNTRIES
REGISTERED TRADEMARK—MARCA REGISTRADA
HECHO EN DRESDEN, TN, U.S.A.

SIGNET, SIGNET CLASSIC, MENTOR, ONYX, PLUME, MERIDIAN
and NAL BOOKS are published *in the United States* by New American Library,
a division of Penguin Books USA Inc., 1633 Broadway,
New York, New York 10019.

First Signet Printing, October, 1989

1   2   3   4   5   6   7   8   9

PRINTED IN THE UNITED STATES OF AMERICA

Contents

Preface

When new medications that were specific for blocking panic attacks first came out, they were hailed as a panacea because they allowed a person to move about more freely. He could go back again and again to those places he feared—without having to worry about a panic attack—until the cycle of sensitization–fear–avoidance was broken.

However well this strategy worked for many patients, it wasn't without a price. First of all, some had unpleasant side effects from the medication. Second, the relapse rate after the medication was stopped was very high; the panic attacks returned in a great many cases.*

Yet many doctors today are still using medication to block the panic attacks prior to exposure therapy simply because they know of no alternative. They are not aware that the panic attacks can be eliminated and the body's chemistry corrected *without resorting to drugs*.

This is why I'm so pleased to introduce you to the program in this book. It presents a viable alternative to medication for panic attack sufferers. This program helps eliminate panic attacks without the possibly hazardous effects of drugs.

I'm a physician; I've been trained in medicine, so I'm

*Pecknold, J.C. and Swinson, R.P. "Taper withdrawal studies with Alprazolam in patients with panic disorder and agoraphobia." *Psychopharmacology Bulletin, 1986*, vol. 22: 173–76
Noyes, R. Jr., Chaudry, D.R., Domingo, D.V. "Pharmacologic treatment of phobic disorders." *J Clinical Psychiatry*, September, 1986, 47:445–52.

not opposed to drugs per se. I prescribe them when I have to. But if a person can recover without drugs— through *natural* means— isn't that much to be preferred?

—SEYMOUR SHEPPARD JAFFE, M.D.

Introduction

Dear Reader,

Let me introduce myself. My name is Shirley Anna Swede, and I'm the founder of PASS-Group.

PASS-Group stands for "Panic Attack Sufferers' Support Group," and also for "We were helped—now we PASS along this help to others." Here's how this organization was started:

For many years I had a problem with recurrent panic attacks. But I found a way to recover. I knew there were a great many people who were suffering as I once did, and I wanted to help them. At that time, the problem of recurrent panic attacks wasn't as well-known among the medical profession, nor was it as widely publicized as it is today.

One day I put a small notice in a neighborhood newspaper. Some of the people who responded were stuck at home, so I began to make "house calls." When it became impossible for me to make personal home visits to all the people asking for help, I began to encourage them over the phone.

Out of that beginning grew the idea of a telephone counseling service for panic attack sufferers. Not a hot line but a three-month course that emphasized the preventive aspects of my methods. In 1981, PASS-Group, Inc. was officially incorporated. Two friends (also recovered panic attack sufferers, whom I'd helped) and I became its first counselors.

This book tells all about the PASS program and about

some of the men and women who have taken it. So this isn't my story alone; it's *our* story.

If you are like most of us who have had panic attacks, you probably feel you are alone and there is no one who could possibly understand how you feel or what you go through. But you're wrong. There is no symptom, no matter how bizarre and frightening it may be to you, that we have not experienced too.

You may feel you are weak to let this thing get the better of you. Perhaps you think you might fight it off and not "let" yourself be this way. Well, that isn't true, either. Sometimes just getting through a bad day takes more courage than anyone who has never experienced a panic attack can imagine.

As far as fighting, you havé been fighting. You just haven't had the right weapons. Tensing up, clenching your teeth and telling yourself, "Oh, no, this time I'm not going to let it happen," only adds fuel to the fire.

So what do you do? What are the weapons? If you're doing this to yourself, how do you stop? This book will provide you with answers.

Remember, no matter how hopeless you may feel your case may be, it isn't. You are now part of a network of people who do understand your problem and what you are going through. And we know there is a cure for you, just as there was for us.

Best wishes and good luck.

Sincerely,

Shirley Anna Swede

PART I

The Fear That Comes from Within

CHAPTER 1

The Pass-Group Program

ACCORDING TO recent surveys, an estimated twelve million Americans are suffering or have suffered, in varying degrees, from recurrent panic attacks. So you're certainly not alone.

In the following pages, we're going to show you what you yourself can do to lessen the chances of getting a panic attack. With our plan for recovery, your panic attacks will diminish in frequency and severity. You'll start going out again and doing those things you are afraid of doing right now.

Going out and doing more and more things will reinforce your courage and hope. Before long, you'll probably be saying to yourself—as so many have done—"Hey, this really isn't so bad, after all. Is this what I was afraid of all these years?"

As you read this book, you'll meet over a dozen people who will tell you their personal stories. They represent a cross-section of the men and women who have been helped by our program. Although each person's story is unique, in many ways the stories are typical. We've included them in the book because we hope they will inspire you to say, "If that person can recover, I can, too!"

Agoraphobia (Panic Disorder) and "Simple" Fears

Before we begin, however, let's clarify certain terms. Agoraphobia (or panic disorder, the newer term) refers to the seemingly spontaneous panic attacks we're talking about here. These terms are often used interchangeably. But it's important to make the distinction between this condition and the so-called simple phobias (i.e., fear of cats, thunder, etc) because these are "outside" fears. Panic disorder, on the other hand, is an "endogenous" fear (meaning, coming from within).

Dr. Claire Weekes, an Australian physician and pioneer in the treatment of panic disorder, was one of the first to recognize this fact—even when many others didn't. "It is the fear of fear within oneself," she wrote. "You are not afraid of the actual places . . . you are afraid you will be unable to cope . . . and what it may lead to." Quite a different matter, she added, from the fear of something "out there."

Thus, panic disorder might cover a whole range of fears including closed-in places, heights, bridges, driving, public speaking, etc. *if* the fear stems from the same source: the fear of having a panic attack in that place or situation.

Why is this distinction so important? Because the origin of these two categories of fear is different. A simple fear—the fear of dogs, for example—might be the result of being bitten by a dog, or having been unduly cautioned about "dangerous dogs." The treatment of simple phobias is pretty straightforward: You recondition the person's reaction through a series of gradual exposures, coupled with relaxation techniques. The first exposure might be to look at a picture of a dog. Later on, the treatment progresses to seeing a small dog at a safe distance, then a bigger dog, and so on until the person's tolerance to dogs is increased.

But endogenous fear is something else. It seems to well up by itself from something inside. So it belongs in a different category and requires a different treatment.

Take a person who's afraid to go down Main Street because he once had a panic attack there. You can't show him a picture of houses and explain that there's really no danger, that the street is safe, etc. He* *knows* there's no

---

*We really mean "he or she," but for the sake of brevity, we use the traditional "he."

danger there. He's just afraid those terrible feelings will come over him again once he's back on the street. So it's not a question of taking him there gradually. He has to be adequately prepared; he has to know about the countermeasures he can take to prevent the panic attacks. Because if he goes to Main Street without that preparation and gets a full-blown panic attack there, he's "sensitizing" himself all over again!

So exposure therapy alone isn't enough. This concept—that there must be an adjunct to the exposure therapy, *something to relieve the panic attacks first*—is now being more widely recognized and accepted, but most therapists are using medication for this purpose. This program presents an alternative. In a great majority of cases, you can get rid of the panic attacks without the use of drugs. This is borne out not only by our observations but by the experiences of other therapists in the field who are using essentially the same methods we're using.

If you're already on medication to block the panic attacks, this program can be used as a means of weaning yourself off the medication, or as a backup safety net when you eventually stop the medication. However, we caution you *not* to stop the drugs abruptly (this may precipitate the panic attacks again), or even to cut down the dosage on your own. You can only do this under your doctor's supervision.

The Underlying Causes

What, actually, is a panic attack?

Panic attacks are distinct episodes of acute fear. Here's how one woman described them: "All of a sudden, for no reason, you're overwhelmed by a feeling of impending doom. Like you're going to die on the spot—or at least, faint. Your chest feels like an elephant is sitting on it. You can't breathe, or else you breathe too much: You hyperventilate. Your heart pounds like a drum. Your hands tremble. Your legs feel like they're made of Jell-O and you think they're going to buckle down under you.

Very often, panic is also accompanied by feelings of unreality. But the most terrifying part is that it seems to be coming out of left field. I mean, you know there's nothing in the immediate environment to cause this—so you think you're going bananas. You're afraid if anyone knew, they'd come and lock you up—so you keep it to yourself. And it becomes a Great Big Secret."

You think, "Maybe if I don't go there, it won't happen." And you often end up inventing excuses why you can't go there. Because—how do you explain it to an outsider? A pattern of avoidance is set up—and in time it becomes a habit.

But what's behind it? Why do these panic attacks come out of the blue, as so many describe them?

The answer is they don't. Typically, this is how the panic attacks start:

1. There is a stress overload for a period of time prior to the onset of the panic attacks.
2. The person is in a run-down condition and poorly nourished for the amount of stress they are carrying. In medical language, being run-down might translate to an enhanced sensitivity to sympathetic nervous system stimuli.
3. The person does too much introspection and worrying about stress-related symptoms.

Many normal people experience some degree of panic from time to time. It might occur during a period of hormonal change such as the onset of puberty or menopause, when studying too hard, or when dieting too strenuously.

But if the person doesn't pay too much attention to panicky feelings and symptoms, the body eventually rights itself. Time, they say, is a great healer, and whatever stress the person is undergoing sooner or later passes. Or, the person somehow learns to adjust. But some people continually ruminate about their symptoms. They don't take proper care of their bodies. They just run from doctor to doctor, looking for a magic cure. If a person worries in secret that the panic attacks are a sure sign of impending insanity or serious illness, then the panic attacks keep coming. Because he's not giving his body a chance to recover.

Your Chance to Recover

A secretary in a college once told us that about fifteen years ago she was in a supermarket when all of a sudden her knees got weak, her heart started to pound, her hands trembled, and she couldn't breathe. She left her wagon of groceries and ran out of the store. The next time she was in the supermarket, the same thing happened. Only worse.

That very evening, she went to see her doctor, who happened to be an old family friend. He examined her carefully and said, "Betty, there's nothing the matter with you. You're just run-down and you need a rest." He prescribed a good diet, some vitamins, exercise—and he sent her home. He also advised her not to go to crowded supermarkets, but to do her shopping when it was not so busy—until she felt better.

She followed his advice, and pretty soon things were back to normal. Eventually, she was able to do her shopping even during crowded times. And she never experienced these episodes again. Now, she jogs, eats well, and enjoys her job.

Yet had her doctor not been as wise and understanding as he was, she would—in all likelihood—have been in treatment for years.

You're probably asking: "If the cure is that simple, then how come so many people suffer? And how come panic attacks can last twenty, thirty—even more—years?"

The answer is that getting into trouble is easier than getting out of it.

When a person is living in constant fear and stress, his body's chemistry changes. The body speeds up the production of stress chemicals. The body, you see, is doing its best to keep up with the demands made upon it. But the more stress chemicals you have, the greater your body's need for certain nutrients—vitamins, minerals, oxygen, etc. If you're too busy worrying and not eating properly, where are these nutrients going to come from? When poor health habits (coupled with poor attitude) become firmly entrenched, they tend to perpetuate themselves. It becomes a vicious cycle. You become trapped, unless you take steps to reverse this process.

Our recovery program will show you how to begin to take those steps, one at a time.

CHAPTER 2

How the Nervous System Works

IN ORDER to gain a better understanding of the nature and origin of panic attacks, it's important to have a basic idea of how the nervous system works. This chapter will give you a nontechnical explanation of some of the forces involved.

Your Nervous System

Your nervous system is divided into two basic categories: the autonomic and the voluntary nervous systems. Your voluntary nervous system is under your direct control, as when you raise your hand. Your autonomic nervous system is *not* under direct control. It is subdivided into the sympathetic and the parasympathetic systems. You would think that the sympathetic one is the calmer of the two because the name suggests something calm and gentle. But it's actually the opposite: The sympathetic nervous system is the one that's aroused when we're angry or frightened. The parasympathetic is the one that calms, that inhibits. In health, both systems operate together in harmony.

The Brain

The brain is roughly divided into three parts: the "logical brain" or outer brain; the "reptilian" or very primitive brain that lies low-down and "sits" over the spinal cord; and the "emotional brain," the interbrain, that lies between the two. In actuality, of course, the functions of the brain are not so neatly divided. All functions are integrated, and there are countless intricate connections between the nerve cells.

The Body's Sentry—the Hypothalamus

In a sense, the hypothalamus heads the autonomic nervous system. It is located in the emotional brain. It is not a large structure (only 3 percent of the total brain weight). Its influence, however, is enormous. Dr. Gustav Eckstein of Harvard calls it the pilot. But it's usually referred to as the body's sentry.

The hypothalamus sounds the alarm to alert the body in case of danger. It sends a message to the pituitary gland—which, in turn, alerts the adrenal glands—and adrenaline (epinephrine) is sent charging into the bloodstream, mobilizing the body.

We all know, of course, that anything that spells danger in the outside environment—like someone pointing a gun at you—will make the sentry sound the alarm. But it's often overlooked that the sentry stands guard over the inner environment, too. In other words, the sentry can pick up clues from the body as well as the mind. Here's how the sentry might become aroused.

The mind: Whenever you believe (it need not necessarily be true) that your existence, your ego, your self-esteem, or your integrity is being threatened—an alarm goes off. *It's your perception that determines your reaction.* Thus, panic attacks can be triggered by *thoughts.*

The body: The triggering factor might be an overactive thyroid, where "all systems go." Or it might even be a severe allergy. *Obviously, you should have a complete physical checkup by your doctor* to rule out any frank physical cause. However, *one of the most common causes* for an inner environment emergency is a blood sugar level that fluctuates too much, that habitually drops too rapidly.

The brain, in order to function normally, needs a constant supply of sugar (glucose) and oxygen. It must have both, because the sugar can only be "burned" (metabolized) in the presence of oxygen; together, they make the energy the cell needs. (It's like when you put gasoline into your car. The fuel is "burned" if oxygen is present, and that's what makes the energy that drives your car.) If not enough sugar is present, there's a problem, and if not enough oxygen is present, there's a problem.* Brain cell metabolism can't proceed—and this is a cause for alarm. The sentry is alerted, and through the chain of command mentioned before, adrenaline is released into the bloodstream.

Now, some of the effects of adrenaline (and there are many) are these: It increases the breathing rate and heart rate, and it makes the body release some of its stored sugar into the bloodstream. The blood sugar level rises; the brain gets what it needs—and it can continue to function.

Yet the side effect of having a lot of adrenaline in the system is the sensation of fear, apprehension—even panic (that's why they call it a panic attack!). As you look around and you see nothing in your environment that's particularly threatening, you might—erroneously—conclude that maybe this means (a) you're dying; (b) you're going crazy; or (c) something really horrible must be going on in your "subconscious." Naturally, this causes even more apprehension and anxiety. (The sentry is now *really* alarmed!) And that means even more fear and more adrenaline.

Yet the panic attack has served a purpose. Looking at it that way, the panic attack may well be a defense mechanism of the body. It may be the by-product of an emergency measure in order to get more blood-carrying

---

*The brain is sensitive to a drop in the sugar level, not the oxygen level. But, if the oxygen level drops, the brain can't use the sugar, either, no matter how much is present.

glucose and oxygen to the brain. The increase in heart rate, breathing, sugar in the blood—all have the effect of rushing to the brain the material it needs to survive. It's almost like a game of chess: You can lose all your pieces, but as long as the king is saved, you're still in the game. As far as your body is concerned, the brain is king!

There are other indications that a panic attack may be Nature's way of getting more sugar into the bloodstream on an emergency basis. High levels of growth hormones have been found in the bloodstream during a panic attack. Growth hormones—aside from helping you grow— also prevent sugar from being deposited in the liver (the major storehouse for sugar). Not only that, but the growth hormone decreases the rate at which sugar is metabolized. The net effect is to increase the available sugar in the bloodstream.

"Well, then," you may say, "if my brain needs more sugar, that's great. Because I do eat a lot of sugar."

No, it isn't great. Because—paradoxically—the more sugar you eat, the *less* your brain gets! Here's why:

Sugar Overload

Everybody's blood sugar level fluctuates somewhat, depending on what you've eaten and when—and the amount of stress or excitement you have. (That's because stress and excitement use up a lot of energy, and sugar supplies energy.) In some people, though, these fluctuations are more erratic; there are greater "highs" and lower "lows."

What makes it this way? And how does it relate to panic attacks? Let's review what we know about the so-called sugar cycle.

All cells use sugar (carbohydrates) for energy. There are two types of sugar: simple sugar (as in the sugar bowl) and complex sugar (as in vegetables and whole grains). Simple sugar is ready to be used "as is" by the body. It doesn't have to be broken down first, because it's already in simple form. Complex sugar, on the other hand, must be broken down before it can be used—and this is done in a series of steps. When you eat foods high in simple sugar ("junk foods"), you're dumping a lot of sugar in all at once. Since it doesn't have to be broken down first, it enters the bloodstream right away—and the sugar level rises too steeply. Now, insulin has to come in to take away the sugar and lead it to the cells. What happens with many people—especially those who have been eating large amounts of sugar for a long period of time—is that the body adapts itself to the greater sugar intake by making it easier for the insulin to be released. The pancreas is "trained" to respond more rapidly, and with greater enthusiasm than necessary. The more insulin that comes in, the more sugar is taken away—and there is a sharper drop in the blood sugar level. At this point, the person begins to feel hungry (usually for sugar foods) and shaky. The body, you see, is calling for more sugar for energy.

If a person hasn't eaten in a while, the body has to dip into its reserves to get the sugar. But in order for the sugar to be released, adrenaline has to come into the picture, because adrenaline holds the key to the sugar storehouses.

If a person has been under stress for a long period of time, he has—unwittingly, perhaps, but similarly—trained his adrenal glands to release a lot of adrenaline, the "fight-or-flight" hormone. Yes, it brings the other side effects of adrenaline: rapid heartbeat, increased breathing, and the intense desire to run, to flee!

As far as blood sugar is concerned, insulin and adrenaline are on opposites sides of a seesaw: Insulin takes away the sugar; adrenaline puts it back.

Under normal conditions, when the person is on a fairly good diet and there's no stress overload, everything works smoothly: sugar (i.e., complex sugar) comes in; insulin takes it away. Then more sugar comes in (if not immediately available from the diet, then from the body's storehouses), and the cycle continues. But it's the combination of stress *and* poor diet (rich in sugar, low in vital nutrients) that plays such havoc with the system. The body simply can't handle all that sugar.

Craving for Sugar

When the body has a requirement for a certain nutrient, it often sends out some sort of message. For example, if you eat a lot of salty foods, you become thirsty. So you drink water, the salt is diluted, and equilibrium is restored.

"So if I crave coffee and cake," you may ask, "doesn't it mean I need sugar?" Yes, you probably do. It usually means the blood sugar level has dropped too low. (Stress uses up a lot of energy!) But here's the catch: If you eat simple sugar (or a heavy meal) you're throwing in a lot of sugar all at once, causing the insulin to come out full force. The more insulin comes in, the more adrenaline has to come in—to balance it out. So it creates a vicious cycle.

This, we think, is why many people fall into the trap of eating sweets (or taking a drink) whenever they feel shaky, tired, depressed, or under stress. (Has this been your pattern, too?) If you eat something with a lot of sugar in it and drink coffee, you feel better right away. Do you see why? The quick energy of the simple sugar and caffeine entered your bloodstream and gave you a temporary lift. If this had happened to you, you probably concluded (logically) that cake, candy, or coffee help you cope. Yet, as you see, although it helps in the short run, in the long run it only makes the problem worse. Because the lift drops with a thud—later. So you're only perpetuating those highs and lows.

The way out of this dilemma is to help stabilize the blood sugar level and keep it on a more even keel. You quiet down the overenthusiastic hormonal responses (the production of insulin and adrenaline) by reducing the amount of stress in your life; by eating a good diet; and by eating small, frequent meals. You substitute complex sugar for simple sugar. Complex sugar takes about four times as long to absorb, so the rise is more gradual, and hence the tapering off is also more gradual.

People react differently to a drop in sugar in the bloodstream. Some will get symptoms, others won't. Out of a group of one hundred "normal" people, maybe about twenty-five will have a "low blood sugar," but only three will develop symptoms, according to a statement by the American Diabetes Association. And even the same individual will respond differently on separate occasions. So it's difficult to establish hard-and-fast rules.

Should you take a glucose tolerance test for hypoglycemia? We don't think it's necessary. (Why bother if the tests are inconclusive anyway?) But if you want to, you can do your own testing. When you feel shaky, drink a small glass of orange juice. If you feel better in a few moments, well, that's probably hypoglycemia!

Hyperventilation

Hyperventilation is the medical term for rapid breathing. When one breathes this way deliberately, it causes temporary symptoms, which can be very frightening to someone who doesn't understand what's happening. The symptoms are: dizziness and lightheadedness; a strong feeling of apprehension; the lips may feel numb; hands and feet lose their coordination; the pulse speeds up; and the heart begins to pound. Thus, every day, in hospital emergency rooms all over the country, people are brought in, hyperventilating, in a state of terror, in what they perceive to be their last moments on earth—only to be told by a doctor that they're in perfect health and just "suffering from nerves."

Breathing, as we all know, brings in oxygen and removes the waste products. But the respiratory system engages in still another very important function: that of regulating the acid-base balance of the body fluids.

Acid and base (alkaline) are chemical opposites. The normal body fluids are slightly on the alkaline side, and they must be maintained that way, within a certain narrow range. The body regulates this balance by withholding or releasing just the right amount of acidity.* How does the body get rid of the excess acid? By throwing it off in the urine—and in the breath.

When you exhale, you give off carbon dioxide and water. Before it becomes carbon dioxide, it's carbonic acid (an *acid*). When you overbreathe (hyperventilate), you're releasing the carbonic acid, so you're turning your body's chemistry more toward the alkaline side. Sometimes overbreathing has to be induced by the automatic nervous system—as, for example, when you have a high fever. During high fever, metabolism increases and there are more (acid) end products of metabolism. The body has to get rid of the excess acid, so the breathing is automatically increased. This corrects the too-high-acid concentration in the blood.

But when over-breathing is done *deliberately*—and many nervous people have a habit of doing this without even realizing it—you are turning your body fluids toward the alkaline side for no good reason. This causes an imbalance between the acid and the base that wasn't there before!

When the body goes too far on the alkaline side, it brings on the symptoms we just mentioned. But remember, these symptoms—however unpleasant—are not dangerous. And they are only temporary. The reason they occur is that when the blood becomes more alkaline, the blood vessels automatically constrict. This limits the amount of oxygen and glucose going to the brain.

These symptoms occur when *anyone* overbreathes; one doesn't have to be a "nervous person" to be so affected (although, if one is nervous, the symptoms can occur more quickly). A number of medical investigators have purposely induced hyperventilation in themselves in order to study its effects on the body. The famous scientist J. B. S. Haldane did this. In an essay called "On Being One's Own Rabbit," he describes how he got

---

*We can almost hear you saying, "But what if it doesn't?" Don't worry. The body has several back-up systems for this; it's fail-safe.

"violent pins-and-needles" in his hands, feet, and face after breathing deeply and rapidly for two to three minutes. He also writes how he once had "continuous spasms" in his hands and face that lasted one and a half hours after a period of self-induced hyperventilation.

Normally, breathing is slow and even. But when there's not enough oxygen in the environment—or if your body's oxygen-carrying capacity is diminished, for whatever reason—the carbon dioxide level in the bloodstream rises. This rise in carbon dioxide triggers the breathing mechanism. In other words, *the body itself initiates the increase in breathing* in order to compensate for the deficit in oxygen.

For example, if you're in a room where there's a higher level of carbon dioxide—let's say, in a room that is poorly ventilated, with a lot of people in it; or if you're in a greenhouse where the carbon dioxide is kept artificially high for the benefit of the plants—your breathing rate is apt to increase. (Remember, it's the carbon dioxide that triggers the breathing mechanism; when it reaches a certain point, the body says, "OK, breathe faster.") A nonphobic person would just take this increased breathing in stride and think nothing of it. But a panic-prone person—an individual who looks inward too much, ready to focus on anything he perceives to be "abnormal" —would be more sensitive to the fact that he is breathing a little faster, and this may have a snowballing effect. The thought: "Oh, my goodness, what's happening to me now—am I starting to get a panic attack again?!" produces fear and an even greater increase in breathing.

Once you understand this, we hope you can at least remain calm *mentally*, even though your breathing may be temporarily increased. We hope you will realize that this is merely the body's attempt to bring in more oxygen and that you won't become unnecessarily frightened by the increased breathing. Because the fear itself might lead to panting and overbreathing, with the attendant temporary disruption of the body's normal biochemistry. (Later on, we'll talk more about the breathing, and show you how you can use it as a means of relaxing yourself.)

Sometimes a little thing like a stuffy nose can bring on a "big" problem with panic attacks. You get panicky feelings when you can't breathe and then you worry why this is happening to you. But *anyone* who feels he can't breathe will react with panic! So when you sense your nasal passages becoming clogged—due to allergies, perhaps—the simple but obvious remedy is to open your mouth a little and breathe. (Later you can look into the problem of allergies.)

Some people, because of prolonged tension and stress, feel their chest muscles are "too tight." So they conclude they have to push their breathing along—otherwise, they think, they may stop breathing altogether. But this is an incorrect assumption. Remember, no one ever committed suicide by holding his breath! You may hold your breath voluntarily until you're literally blue in the face and faint. But eventually you'll breathe. Why? Because carbon dioxide will accumulate in the bloodstream, and when it reaches a certain level it will stimulate the respiratory center in the brain and you'll resume breathing. That's the miracle of the body's biochemistry at work.

Here's another interesting fact about breathing: The more attention you pay to your breathing, the more irregular it becomes. (When I (SAS) was in nursing school, we had to check each other's pulse and respiration. As soon as we knew our breathing was being observed, the normal rhythm became disturbed. This happened to many of us in the class; it was hard to get an accurate measurement.)

So you have to allow your body to do its job; you have to trust your body more. It knows what it's doing. After all, it's been breathing since you were born.

Sodium Lactate Infusion

Back in 1967, doctors at the Washington University School of Medicine demonstrated that it was possible to regularly induce a panic attack in patients who had previously complained of spontaneous panic attacks. When the doctors administered sodium lactate intravenously, the patient would experience all the agonizing symptoms of a panic attack. This seldom happened to others, who might only experience mild symptoms, such as numbness and/or muscle tremors (sodium lactate is an alkalizing agent).

Since sodium lactate is a normal by-product of cell metabolism, we can infer that the people who respond with panic might simply be more sensitive to the buildup of this chemical. Or that sodium lactate isn't being removed from the system at the proper rate. Or that the level of sodium lactate is already high in a person who is subject to panic attacks, and that this additional infusion merely throws him over the edge, setting the stage for a full-blown panic attack.

But why, you ask, would the sodium lactate level be high in the first place?

Let's talk for a moment about muscle activity. Muscles are normally slightly contracted. This is called muscle tone. During sleep, when the body is relaxed, there is very little muscle tone. But during waking hours there is always some muscle contraction going on. (Otherwise, how would you be able to sit or stand?) A very nervous person, one who jumps at the slightest noise, would have a great deal more muscle tone, because his muscles would be doing a lot more contracting; they'd all be keyed up. Now, in order to perform, muscles need oxygen. So it stands to reason that a person who is very tense most of the time will use up more oxygen than someone who is relatively relaxed.

Whenever muscles are made to work (i.e., to contract) without enough oxygen being present, a chemical called lactic acid starts to collect around the muscles. Muscles don't like to have lactic acid hanging around; it literally cramps their style. It makes them ache and feel fatigued. So the body has to get rid of the lactic acid. How? By breaking it down, ultimately into carbon dioxide and water. But in the process of breaking it down chemically, sodium lactate is produced. Therefore, if you have a lot of lactic acid to begin with, isn't it reasonable to suppose that there would be a lot of sodium lactate as well, since the latter represents a chemical reaction produced by the breakdown of lactic acid?

So what it boils down to is this: Science has finally confirmed that nervous, sensitive people are more likely to get panic attacks!

And yet, understanding the underlying chemistry gives us a better handle on the problem:

1. You can increase your body's ability to process oxygen more efficiently (making the most of each breath, so to speak).
2. You can teach your body to conserve oxygen by decreasing your body's need for oxygen.
3. You can enhance your body's ability to get rid of excess lactic acid.

Fortunately, all of the above can be achieved through the integrated steps presented in this program. Since each helps the other, the *combined* approach is far more effective than any single method alone.

The Fear Center in the Brain

Experiments with laboratory animals show that when an electrode (an electrical stimulus) is applied to a certain part of the hypothalamus, the animal reacts with acute fear or rage. More recently, a series of experiments were performed at another brain site called the locus coeruleus (suh-rool-ee-us), which we'll call the LC. The LC is much smaller than the hypothalamus. But it also has a very important role, since virtually all important brain structures, including the hypothalamus, are connected to it in some way.

When Eugene Redmond of Yale wired the brains of monkeys and electrically shocked them at the LC point, the monkeys exhibited their equivalent of what in humans would have been a panic attack. So it may very well be that the first panic-button-pusher is the LC—and the panic may be brought about by nerves firing off at this location instead of—or along with—the hypothalamus. But whatever the final research shows, the theoretical concept is still the same: The feeling of panic is being triggered by bursts of electricity deep within the brain.

The EEG that we use to measure brain activity—although it can pick up signals emanating from the *outer* layers of the brain—is not sensitive enough to pick up signals that come from within the deeper, interior parts of the brain. Such signals are weak to begin with, and, in addition, must pass through many layers of tissue and bone before they reach the "outside" where they can be measured. Thus, direct evidence of electrical misbehavior in the LC or hypothalamus is lacking; however, we infer—as we always do from analogous experiments with animals—that this is indeed what is happening in the human brain.

But it must also be understood that these local sites, however interesting they are to the researcher, to you, to us, are not isolated sites in the sense that they signal, "Aha, we have found the culprit!" Their influence extends, by means of a complicated network, to all major parts of the brain. And, of course, the brain is connected to the body. So we always have to keep an eye on the total picture—instead of just a tiny part.

Does this mean that the LC has "usurped" the hypothalamus's role as the body's sentry? Some researchers think so. They've called the LC the alarm system of the brain. But whether it's the LC or the hypothalamus, is, for our purposes, relatively unimportant. The basic concept—namely that there is in the brain some coordinating mechanism that functions as a guardian or sentry that can trigger the fight-or-flight response—is still the same.

The LC also seems to act as a regulating device that can turn up or turn down all stimuli—much like the knob on a radio that controls the volume.

The Endorphins

Additional studies of the LC reveal that it is richly

endowed with opiate receptors. Opiate receptors are nerve cell receptors that only accept chemicals resembling opium and opium derivatives like morphine. This was an astounding discovery. How could the body know that opium would ever be used? The discovery led to an intensive search for some naturally occurring substances that would chemically resemble the structure of opium. And finally such substances were found. They were named endorphins.

Here's what the endorphins do. They diminish pain, anxiety, and fear; enhance the immune system of the body (hence the ability to withstand stress); and lower the threshold for pleasure—which means it makes it easier for any pleasurable stimuli to get through.

The endorphins and opiate receptors are chemically complimentary. One fits into the other, like a key in a lock. So, to put it in the very simplest of terms, the endorphins plug up the holes in the fear center of the brain, so the fear doesn't come out!

The discovery that there is a fear center in the brain and that the fear center is richly supplied with opiate receptors is a very significant one, because this information now gives us yet another handle, a way of dealing with the fear response. It shows that there is a way of turning down the volume, so to speak, of a "hyper" nervous system—through the increased production of endorphins.

CHAPTER 3

Conditions Associated with Panic Disorder

A NUMBER OF popular theories link certain conditions and/or symptoms with panic disorder. Let's examine some of them and see how they relate to panic attacks.

Mitral Valve Prolapse (MVP)

Among those who suffer from panic disorder, the percentage who also have MVP is significantly higher than among the general population. More women than men have MVP. It seems to be inherited.

How is MVP, an anatomical imperfection in the heart, related to panic attacks?

Let's review the anatomy. The heart is divided into four chambers: left, right, upper, and lower. The mitral valve separates the heart's upper and lower chambers on the left side of the heart. The blood passes the mitral valve as it moves from the upper chamber to the lower. Normally, this passage is a one-way route: The valve opens up, allows the blood to flow through, then closes tightly to prevent a backflow. However, if there's a slight defect in the valve so it can't close tightly, a small amount of blood may seep back through, to the upper chamber. This condition is generally considered benign; the imperfection in the valve might be of no more significance than imperfectly spaced teeth. A statement by the New York Heart Association is very reassuring: The condition does not seem to be a cause of heart attacks.

You can readily see that at times, especially during stress, not enough blood may be getting through to the brain fast enough. This could cause a temporary dizziness or feeling of lightheadedness. The body, in an effort to send more blood to the brain, speeds up the heart rate. But the mind, at this point, might also signal a red alert: What person wouldn't be frightened if he thinks he's having a heart attack?

If you're worried about possible heart problems, for your own peace of mind, you should see your doctor.

We want to add this, though. The heart is a muscle. And, like any muscle in the body, it can be strengthened through exercise. As the heart gets stronger, the heart can afford to slow down, because now the heart is able to squeeze more blood through with every beat, every thump. And this means more oxygen and more food to all the cells, including, of course, the brain cells. A deconditioned heart, on the other hand—one that's weak through lack of exercise—must keep beating faster and faster, especially during stress. The heart just doesn't have the power to squeeze through, with one swoosh, any great amount of blood, so it has to do it with many tiny beats to keep up. Obviously, a stronger heart would insure a better blood supply and diminish the episodes of dizziness.

Problems of the Inner Ear

Another condition with a high correlation to panic attacks is trouble with the inner ear. That's where the body's balancing mechanism lies. There's always fluid there, and when we move or turn our heads, the fluid moves, too, to maintain its level position (it's like tilting a glass of water). From this information, the sensitive nerve-endings in that area pick up the message regarding the body's position and relay it to the brain. The brain then sends messages to the various muscles—and that's how the body maintains its balance.

However, if there's some swelling in the inner ear (due to infection, allergy, and so forth), the fluid increases and presses against sensitive nerves. The message gets garbled; it's as if you were on the high seas. This brings on a giddiness and nausea that can range from a slight feeling of being off-balance to the sensation of seeing the room spinning around like a merry-go-round—only it's not so merry.

The ground may appear to be wavy or as if it's buckling under. There may be episodes of lightheadedness, dizziness, feeling unsteady on the feet, or having the impression of tilting to one side while walking. These sensations can trigger panic attacks in sensitive individuals—especially if you don't know what's happening and assume the worst. True, lightheadedness can be a manifestation or symptom of the panic attack itself, but it can also be the cause of it. Remember we spoke earlier of how the sentry stands guard over the inner environment, too? A sense of disequilibrium in the body— particularly if it occurs suddenly—can make that sentry sound the alarm.

Sometimes this condition is referred to as Ménière's syndrome, but, actually, Ménière's is characterized by three conditions: dizziness, ringing in the ears, and hearing loss.

Elevators, escalators, cars, buses, planes, and boats are common places for a panic attack. Getting panic attacks in places associated with motion should raise the suspicion of an inner-ear involvement. Consult an ear-nose-and-throat specialist (otolaryngologist) to rule out or confirm this condition. But don't worry—it's treatable. A salt-free diet is usually recommended, with or without medication.

Premenstrual Syndrome

During the premenstrual period, many women suffer from a combination of symptoms caused by water retention. The excess fluid also irritates the nervous system, which accounts for the feelings of inner shakiness, a tendency to fly off the handle, and panic attacks, if one is predisposed to having them. The blood sugar level tends to be more unstable at this time, too, so many women get strong cravings for sweets just before their period. What you can do is have more complex carbohydrates at this time—and pay even closer attention to your diet and vitamin supplements. You can also take frequent, brief exercise breaks.

The standard non-drug treatment of PMS—a good diet, exercise, stress-reduction, salt-restriction, and so on—is exactly what we will be recommending for panic attack recovery.

Enzyme Impairment?

Besides increased adrenaline and insulin production, some researchers have found, in their studies of a group of panic attack sufferers, some impairment of enzyme activity related to carbohydrate metabolism (i.e., the way the body burns sugar).

What are enzymes? They're substances that make chemical reactions possible; they're catalysts. Enzymes need certain vitamins to help them do their job (vitamins are often called co-enzymes, i.e., vitamin-helpers). Without vitamins in the right amounts, the enzymes can't work properly. As we've already said, one of the by-products of carbohydrate metabolism is lactic acid. Therefore, if metabolism doesn't proceed normally, lactic acid will tend to accumulate. And this can trigger panic attacks in susceptible people.

Why might this enzyme system become impaired? It might be the result of years of poor diet (i.e., eating foods whose vitamins and other nutrients have been removed through commercial processing) and/or a higher inborn requirement for certain vitamins. Whatever the cause, this condition does seem to be reversible. Common sense would dictate that the aim of the therapy could be to correct the underlying malfunctioning enzyme activity, through good nutrition and vitamin supplementation.

In our experience, large doses were not needed—

probably because we use a total, holistic approach and because each facet of the program helps restore proper balance and health. In any case, megadoses of vitamins (or any other nutrient) should *not* be taken without adequate supervision by a professional who is knowledgeable in nutrition. In megadoses, vitamins act like drugs.

A Chemical Imbalance

There has been much furor and controversy lately about whether the panic attacks are the result of emotional factors or whether they're the result of chemical imbalance. Those who favor the emotional factors want to treat panic disorder with behavior modification; those who favor the physical component want to treat it with drugs.

Anything that stimulates the overproduction of hormones (adrenaline, insulin, enzymes, etc.) creates an imbalance, a disturbance in the body's chemistry. We're all chemical factories, in a sense. You literally couldn't lift a finger without a chemical reaction taking place! Foods are chemicals, too. Think about it. These entities—plants, animals, eggs, fish—were once alive. And now, when you eat them, they are mechanically and chemically broken down by your body for your own use. The energy locked in those foods is released and passed on to you when you eat them.

So if you're not getting the right foods that your body needs, won't there be a chemical imbalance? If your lactate level builds up too much (because you're too tense all the time or because your carbohydrates aren't being metabolized properly or because your oxygen-carrying capacity is underdeveloped)—isn't there a chemical imbalance? If you (or anyone else) start to overbreathe and the body's acid-base balance is temporarily disturbed—that's a chemical imbalance, too, isn't it? If your body is producing too many stress chemicals because you're overworked—or because you're thinking of danger all the time—what does that do to your body's chemistry?

Yet, many people assume when they hear the phrase, chemical imbalance, there is some missing-link chemical—and if only they could get their hands on it, they'd be cured!

Sure, certain drugs have been found to be helpful in blocking the panic. However, with drugs, you always have to consider the possibility of undesirable side effects. Some of these drugs are relatively new, so no one knows what the long-term side effects might be. In addition, when you stop the drugs, the panic attacks may return.

Certainly, it is far better to correct the chemical imbalance through natural means—through diet, exercise, stress-management and a positive attitude. These are the methods we used in our program for the past several years, with excellent results.

Now, we're not taking the position that medication should never be used. But it should be used as a last resort, not as a first choice. If there are other options available, why take unnecessary medication?

Why Are There More Women Sufferers?

Why are there so many more women who suffer from agoraphobia? Dr. Claire Weekes reports that less than 10 percent of her patients were men. Yet in our experience, some years later, closer to 30 percent of the people we have helped are men. We attribute this increase to the newer attitudes about male/female roles. Men today are not as reluctant to admit they're afraid. They're a lot more open about it. We even feel that many more men have panic attacks but mask them with alcohol. The physical reason often given for alcoholism is a recurrent lowering of the blood sugar level—certainly something very similar to what seems to be happening in panic disorder.

There may be other reasons why women are especially prone to agoraphobia. Girls generally have a more receptive, waiting attitude than boys. If there's danger out there, they're not as apt to run to meet it head on. (As Gloria Steinem once remarked, "Women don't have to prove anything.") So they can more easily fall into the habit of avoiding if they choose to emphasize the "dangerous" aspect of going out. Boys, on the other hand, have a different orientation. Testosterone, the male hormone, creates in young men much more of a drive to go out, to do, to meet danger. Boys also tend to be more active physically. In young women, poor nutrition and poor physical conditioning can have a bad effect on the glandular system, particularly the menstrual cycle. As we have seen, this can cause swelling in the brain and other tissues prior to menstruation, making the panic attacks more likely to come at this time.

So all these factors may weight the balance "in favor" of women.

Yet it's interesting to note, in passing, that the German physician, Dr. Westphal, who in 1871 coined the term, agoraphobia, did so after he encountered in his practice three patients who were afraid to go to the center of town. All three patients were men!

CHAPTER 4

How to Prepare Yourself for the Program

You HAVE just seen how a number of factors, working together, can stir up the nervous system into an upward spiral of chaos. By using the same principle—a number of factors, all working together—you can reverse this spiral. You can make it go in the opposite direction.

How do you go about calming a nervous system that you can't reach directly, that's not under voluntary control? The answer, of course, is that you have to do it indirectly.

Our program of recovery consists of the following seven components:

1. Diet
2. Relaxation
3. Exercise
4. The Right Attitude
5. Imagination
6. Social Support
7. Spiritual Values

We ask that you do not start going out to those places and situations you fear the most until you have been following the program long enough to feel physically stronger, calmer, more adequate. Naturally, this timespan varies with each individual, but in most cases it's about six to eight weeks. If you had a broken leg, you wouldn't run right away, would you? So you have to allow time for your body/mind to heal also.

The panic attacks are stress-related, so anything you

can do to alleviate the stresses in your life will be of great help. Most of us, thank goodness, don't have to face life-or-death emergencies on a daily basis. Most often, it's the accumulation of the little stresses that gets us down. That's why it's important to give thought to how your daily life is structured.

Think of your day-to-day activities as a continuum that goes from one extreme to the other:

No Activity	*Too Much Activity*
Boring,	Frantic, agitated,
Stifling	distraught

Either extreme—too much as well as too little activity— is very stressful to the human body. Obviously, most of us would be more comfortable somewhere around the center—but whether it's a little more to the right or left of that center is strictly an individual preference.

The idea, of course, is to work out a balance that's right for you. Where would you feel more comfortable?

If you have a strenuous job either at home with small children or in the business world, it's important to balance it with quiet, restful activities at certain times during the day. You don't save the pent-up frustrations and then go on a two-week-long holiday. Balance your activities on a daily basis. If you don't have the time, then make the time. It's your health and happiness that are at stake.

Say, for example, you're a free-lance writer, working at home. Writing is lonely; it's also sedentary work. So, in order to create a balance, you have to find company. You have to do some activity that involves walking, exercise, and so on. A mini-vacation for you might be to close shop and go visit a friend. Or go jogging in the park for a while with a friend. If, on the other hand, you have a busy workday—seeing a lot of people or going to meetings, for example—a mini-vacation for you might be to take time out and curl up with a good book, work on a stamp collection, or paint. Being with people all day long, adjusting to novel situations or getting a lot of input can be very tiring day after day. Your mind needs rest and relief.

Pleasure Island

One of the most effective ways to relieve daily stress is to create "pleasure islands" during the day. Some little activity that you enjoy doing—if even for a few moments at a time.

For example, I (SAS) was recently under a lot of stress. My mother was in the hospital, needing surgery. So whenever I went to the hospital, I would stop by a pleasant little coffee shop and relax there a bit with a hot cup of tea and something I'd bring to eat from home. I would take along a book to read on the bus, on the way to the hospital. I'd chat with friends on the telephone. When I'd come home, I'd romp around with my dog in the backyard for half an hour—as my exercise for the day. I'd go to the park or some other quiet nature place as often as I could. I'd visit friends. I also designed and made sketches of art work I would later do.

You have to create for yourself, too, little islands of pleasure when surrounded by a sea of stress. Unrelieved stress and tension—without respite and without relief—cannot do you or your family any good.

Tuning Out

Many people have a habit of turning on the radio for the news and weather first thing in the morning. This is a very bad practice. The news is always bad, and when you hear it in the morning, it sets your mood for the day. If you must listen to something in the morning, tape some nice music and listen to that. Or something uplifting and cheerful. (You can always find out about the weather by dialing a certain number—ask your local information operator.)

Some people ask: "But if I don't listen to the news, how would I know what's going on in the world?" There are four billion humans in the world today. That means billions of events, good and bad, are happening all over the world. But the media people select only the news they want you to hear. They don't tell you that a woman on your block had a wonderful evening with friends. They don't tell you that so-and-so finally got his long-awaited promotion. They don't tell you anything about ordinary people, who are just living their lives.

And yet many people think they know everything because they read the papers and listen to the news . . . or, conversely, that they won't know anything if they stop listening.

Those of us who are prone to panic attacks are highly susceptible to our environment—good *or* bad. We're highly suggestible. That's why you benefit so much by feeding your mind positive thoughts instead of negative thoughts.

An Old Wound

Sometimes there's a lot of stress in your present life because you focus too much attention on an old, hurtful event that may have happened long ago. It becomes like a scab that's constantly being picked on. You don't give your wound a chance to heal.

That's why Dr. Weekes's "four principles"—face; accept; float (in the sense of: ease up a little, let go, don't hold on to the hurt so tightly); and let time pass—work very well here, also. We might just add one more principle—to allow other interests, other friends, other experiences, to enter your life. Because those beneficial influences can be the very ointment you need for your wound, to help it heal.

You're far less apt to be resentful, less inclined to ponder about the injustices done to you, when your life is filled with good things.

The Worry Hour

Many people are champion worriers. They've had so much time to practice! What I tell them is this: Set aside a certain time to worry. I call it the worry hour. Do all

your worrying only during that time. Leave the rest of
the day free for other pursuits. Whenever a particular
worry comes to mind, you don't have to say, "Oh, I
mustn't think of it, I mustn't have that stress," etc. You
can say to yourself, "I'll think about it later. At 4 P.M."
(But don't be surprised if you can't keep your mind on
your worry for that whole hour!)

Look for the Good

You've heard this expression many times before: "It's
the little things in life that count." So why not try this:
For one month, keep a "Diary of Beautiful Things."
Record the little things you see every day that are beautiful, that reach out to you. For example, the way the sun
shines on a piece of glass, the color of a flower, the way
someone smiles at you, etc. Learn to find pleasure in the
commonplace things around you.

Sometimes, when we're confronted by ordinary stressful life situations and personality clashes, it may seem as
if there's nothing we can ever do to change it. And yet, a
positive way of thinking and looking for the good, can
often work wonders.

For example, here's what one client told us:

> I used to have a lot of stress on my job. And mainly it
> was because I was working next to this girl I didn't like.
> I just couldn't stand her. I used to be so irritated by
> everything she said and did. But then one day—I don't
> know how this idea came to me, but I thought of this: No
> one can be all bad or all good. So I said to myself, there
> must be something good about this person. And I began to
> look for it. I began to search out the good qualities. And
> I did find several things about her that I liked. So I kept
> concentrating on those things. And then a miracle hap-
> pened. This girl became a lot more friendly towards me! I
> guess she sensed that I liked her more, so she began to
> like me. And so our friendship started to grow.
>
> Now things are so much better on the job. It's a plea-
> sure coming in to work in the morning because I don't
> have all this negativity around me anymore. I feel better.

And I also feel a little proud of myself, too. Because I know I was the one who took the initiative to change things around.

Having a Goal

Everyone needs a goal, something to strive for. To accomplish. To look forward to. I've (SSJ) seen people in nursing homes languish and deteriorate rapidly—not only because of their age—but because they had nothing to look forward to, nothing to work toward. Everything was done for them; all they had to do was eat and sleep. People need more than that. The human being was designed to exert himself on his behalf, to overcome obstacles, to solve problems. This is good stress, as Dr. Selye, the world renowned researcher on stress, would have said.

What are some of your goals? Would you like to start a business of your own? Would you like to finish your schooling? Do you have some unfinished business that you'd like to take care of?

Life Thoughts

We all know it's important to develop a more cheerful attitude and to dwell more on the cup being half-full instead of half-empty.

But this is not to say that you must never, ever ponder about the sadness in life. These thoughts come to any thinking, sensitive person from time to time. They're part of life. But it's important to realize that this is what it means to be a human being, and that you were not singled out by Providence to be the only person in the world to suffer.

You may remember the old tale about a young woman who lost her newborn son. Her grief was so great that she came to a wise man and begged him to give her an instant cure for her sorrow. The wise man told her she would have to wear, for only one day, the hair-ribbons of a woman who had never grieved. Although she searched everywhere, she could never find such a woman. At last she realized that her troubles were not so very different from anyone else's. Her sorrow lifted when she knew she was not alone.

I once read, a long time ago in one of Pearl S. Buck's books, about a young handmaiden who falls in love with her master's son. She knows full well he can never marry her, and the thought saddens her. She begins to ask herself many questions. She wonders: Is life meant to be sad or happy? She concludes that life is inherently sad; that one can never get all desires fulfilled. But, paradoxically, this thought gives her contentment. She knows she's not the only one who has to suffer.

Sometimes clients tell me they're afraid of dying. (I answer, I'm not so crazy about it myself.) But very often the fear of dying masks an emptiness in life. Psychologist Lawrence LeShan, who did a lot of research on the reactions of terminally ill patients once told the story of a woman he visited in the hospital. This patient was dying of cancer, and while he was interviewing her, she burst into tears. He assumed this was because she was dying and he tried to comfort her. "No," she said, "I'm not crying because I'm going to die soon. I'm crying because I never lived!"

When you have a reason to live, when you have a task that you want very much to accomplish, when you can hardly wait for a new day to dawn so you can go about your work, the fear of dying falls away.

Dr. Rochelle Myers, a well-known California psychologist, once said, "Most people tiptoe through life trying to reach death safely." They're so overcautious that they don't really live.

Don't let this happen to you.

Seven Antistress Tips

1. Don't waste time trying to change somebody. It doesn't work. The only person you can change is yourself.
2. Do one thing at a time. Doing several things at once may be a source of pride, but it is also a source of stress.
3. Maintain a variety of interests, and friends, so when things go wrong in one area, you always have another.
4. If you have a particularly vexing problem to solve, it's very helpful to write it out. The very act of having to put it down on paper helps to clarify your thoughts. And once the problem is identified, it becomes easier to solve: "A problem well-stated is a problem half-solved."

   When you have the problem written out, list all your options. First—do it right off the top of your head, without being judgmental about whether it'll work or not. After you have written as many options as you can think of, go back and write your comments about each one. After your evaluation, select the one that's best. Sometimes, though, none of the options are too palatable. In that case, you strike out those you absolutely don't want—and work with what's left.
5. Another method of problem-solving (once the problem is identified) is to let your subconscious do the work. With this method, you don't try to solve the problem; you only go about getting the facts. You just fill your mind with all sorts of facts you can dig up that relate (directly or indirectly) to the problem. Then, one day—when you least expect it (i.e., when your mind is resting lightly on other things)—a solution may suddenly present itself.

   If no answer comes, maybe you're asking the wrong question. There are some questions that cannot be answered (like the "Why me?" question). So, restate the question; try to see it from a different angle.

6. Get in the habit of breaking up problems into smaller, more manageable pieces. Remember: "One step is enough for me."

7. Get involved in creative work—something that will occupy your imagination to the fullest and make you jump out of bed in the morning, eager to start your day.

Remember, when you're in better physical shape, when you're better nourished and no longer run-down, when your body has been buoyed up by a positive attitude, then you are better able to tolerate the stresses of life.

Listening to Your Doctor

As we mentioned earlier, occasional panic attacks are common. They can happen to almost anyone when we're overtired, overstressed, and run-down. But an occasional panic attack isn't a sickness. Dr. David H. Barlow, professor of psychology at the State University of New York at Albany, recently gave a lecture at a phobia conference. "In any given year," he said, "probably up to 30-40 percent of the population have panic attacks."*

What perpetuates the attacks? What keeps them going? Why are so many people suffering?

There are a constellation of factors at work here: There's usually a lifestyle or environment that leads to isolation and preoccupation with the Self. This intensifies and feeds on any hypochondriac tendencies—that is, a penchant for listening in to bodily functions. It's true that when a person is under stress *and* run-down (in other words, when the parasympathetic nervous system is tem-

*See: Norton, G.R., Harrison, B., Hauch, J., Rhodes, L. "Characteristics of people with infrequent panic attacks." *J Abnormal Pscyhology*, 1985, vol. 94, No. 2; 216–21, Norton, G.R., Dorward J., Cox, B.J. "Factors associated with panic attacks in non-clinical subjects." *Behavior Therapy*, 1986, 17: 239–52.

porarily subdued and the sympathetic nervous system takes over), bodily functions *are* more evident. The stress chemicals that are being manufactured more abundantly activate the nerve endings in various organs in the body. Thus, heart sounds seem louder, the rumbling in the intestines becomes magnified, and so on. So, in a sense, you can't help but notice these things and become concerned. All we can say is this: Let your doctor be your guide. If he says you're healthy, believe it. If your doctor assures you that no, you don't have heart trouble; no, you don't have a brain trumor; no, there's nothing the matter with your throat, believe it. As you follow the program, as you learn to relax more easily, your nervous system will regain its balance and these symptoms will subside.

Letting Go of Being Perfect

Then there is the matter of wanting to be perfect, another common trait among people who suffer from recurrent panic attacks. In this context, perfection means expecting the body/mind to function faultlessly all the time, so any deviation from the norm becomes a cause for alarm. This quest for perfection becomes an additional source of stress when it overflows into other areas (as it usually does). For example, a person always wants things to be just so, and becomes angry and frustrated when they're not. He may expect family and friends to be perfect also. He may hold back from entering situations where a panic attack might be embarrassing ("What if I make a fool of myself?"). Meaning: How can I show all these people that I'm not perfect? The result of this unrealistic and rigid expectation is a poor self-image, which obviously leads to even more stress.

Some researchers even believe that the striving for perfection (and the constant disappointments) are at the root of the emotional aspects of panic disorder. So it's certainly worth asking yourself: Why strive for something that may be causing harm?

Remember, we're not saying you shouldn't strive for excellence. But there's a difference between striving for perfection and striving for excellence. If you strive for perfection, you berate yourself if things aren't perfect. If you strive for excellence and things aren't perfect, don't berate yourself—simply correct the error the next time. Be willing to learn from experience, but don't put yourself down.

The Fear of Going Crazy

So many people who suffer from panic attacks secretly fear they're going crazy. They fear they'll run around screaming and tear their clothes off in public or throw their kids out the window. They're sure that when their anxiety reaches a certain level, they'll crack up and carry out these dreaded deeds. Yet, as Dr. Manuel D. Zane, the well-known researcher on panic disorder, once quipped, "If you don't think a lot of crazy things, you're not in this world." It's natural for the mind to wander into a labyrinth of crazy thoughts when it is overtaxed and the body is run-down.

The other day, I was talking to a new client and she said, "I can go anywhere in my own town, but as soon as I try to go to the next town, I get those terrible feelings. I see something awful happening to me. Like I get into an accident. Or the car breaks down. Or somebody trying to break into my car. [Wouldn't anybody be frightened by such vivid images?] I *know* I shouldn't think of these things," she continued, "and *I try so hard not to*. But I can't help it. They just come to me."

"Suppose," I said to her, "I tell you *not* to think of a white elephant for the next five minutes. Don't, under any circumstances, in any shape or form, think of a white elephant . . . What comes to your mind?" She paused and I could "hear" her smile over the phone. "A white elephant," she replied. If you try very hard *not* to think crazy thoughts, that's practically a guarantee that they'll come. It's a paradox: The more you try *not* to think of something, the more it clings to you. (It's often said that the best way to remember something is to try very hard to forget it.) This woman tried so hard not to worry that she ended up worrying even more!

People under great stress may *think* a lot of crazy things, but that doesn't mean they're going to do anything about it; thinking and doing are two separate issues. The cases you read about in the paper, where someone runs amok, are *not* applicable to you, the panic attack sufferer. Those people have serious mental illnesses of a *psychotic* nature. Psychosis is something else entirely. Psychosis does not *ever* turn into an anxiety disorder or a neurosis. These are two separate categories.

Dr. Richard O. Anderson, a psychiatrist who practices in Minneapolis, once told me that in order to let this idea sink in with his patients, he asks them this question: "How long can a person have pneumonia before it turns into lung cancer?" The correct answer, of course, is never; they're two separate problems. But some patients will answer, "six months." Or "a year." So he has another question up his sleeve. "How long does it take," he asks, "for a dog to turn into a cat?" At this point, the patient usually begins to smile; he gets the point.

Never Saying "I'm Phobic"

Many people use the term "phobic" in describing themselves. They'll say, "I'm phobic" or "I'm agoraphobic." (One of these days I expect to see coffee mugs with the inscription, "Kiss me, I'm phobic.") Or they'll refer to the panic attacks as "my agoraphobia."

After the deluge of publicity on agoraphobia, many were so relieved to know that—finally—"it" has a name. Yet we say this: Don't get so hung up on a name that you identify too closely with it. Once you give yourself a label, you box yourself into a certain category, a certain mind-set. It becomes a self-fulfilling prophecy and it makes it difficult for you to change. You expect to act a certain way, so you do act a certain way. But if you free yourself from the negative label and think of yourself as being in a state of transition (which you are), you're in a much better position to experiment, to try new things. If you keep referring to it as "my" agoraphobia, it'll begin to sound like an affectionate term—and you wouldn't want to part with it!

First Fear and Second Fear

One of the most important contributions in the management of panic disorder was made by Dr. Claire Weekes when she theorized that the panic attack actually comes in two stages. She calls these stages First Fear and Second Fear.

By First Fear, she means the sudden fear that comes unbidden—out of the blue. Second Fear is your reaction to it. It's what you tell yourself about it. It's characterized by self-sentences like: "Oh, my goodness, not again . . .!"; "Oh, this is terrible—I'm surely dying this time . . . !"; "Oh, why is all this happening to me . . .?!"; "It'll just keep getting worse and worse, and never stop . . ."

Why is this such an important observation? Because in breaking up the problem this way, it becomes much more manageable. You can then begin to deal with each of the components as separate issues.

Many people believe that First Fear can be stopped with nothing less than very powerful drugs. But, in our experience, this is not so. There *are* ways to stop or prevent First Fear.

Let's quickly review: As we've said, the panic attacks are initially brought about under the following circumstances:

1. The (susceptible) person had been under stress for a long period of time (before the panic attacks began).
2. The (susceptible) person had been in a run-down condition (resulting from poor health habits) and was therefore unable to handle that stress load.

But when you raise the level of health—and, at the same time, you decrease the stresses in your life (either by changing the situation or by changing your attitude toward the situation), First Fear diminishes in frequency and intensity—or it disappears altogether.

So you *do* have control of First Fear. (You control it through the voluntary choices you make regarding your lifestyle.)

Therefore, you needn't fear the panic attacks as much—because the panic attacks will, in almost all cases (i.e., if they're still around), become mere shadows of their former selves.

Yes, shock is a very powerful learning tool. That's why you've learned to avoid certain places and situations. That's why when Dr. Weekes says to accept the shock and "let the panic come and do its worst," it's very hard not to flinch! But what we're telling you is that the shock *now*, even if it does come, will, in all probability* *not* be as strong as it used to be—and you can handle it. It takes—what? A few seconds? A minute? A few minutes? The shock waves die down on their own.

Dr. Weeks writes: ". . . [The agoraphobic] should be taught that panic can come only in a wave and must always die down if he but waits and does not fall into the trap of stoking his fires with Second Fear . . . [Without Second Fear] the panic *will not mount*."

This is most reassuring: "The panic will not mount." Excellent. Well, then, if the panic will not mount—if the worst has *already* happened—what is there to be afraid of?

You can readily see that whenever you add Second Fear, you only intensify First Fear. It's like standing near a quiet pond and throwing in a pebble. You watch the ripples spread—then grow fainter and fainter—until they all disappear and the pond is calm again. But if you keep on throwing in more pebbles, how can it quiet down?

Often, when I'm discussing, Dr. Weekes's books with clients, they refer to this statement, ". . . true acceptance

*That is, if you've been following the program for a while.

means to be prepared to let the panic come and do its worst and not withdraw from it . . ." And they ask me with trepidation: "But how can I practice true acceptance of the panic attacks when they're so horrible?"

With all due respect to Dr. Weekes and her wonderful work, in our experience, the diet, the exercise, the relaxation, and certainly, a better attitude significantly reduce the chances of a panic attack. Once you gain a better understanding of how the nervous system works, once you realize that the nervous system cannot be forced and that you must use a different strategy, you begin to gain the real control you're seeking.

PART II

The 7-Step Program

CHAPTER 5

Step 1: Diet

"Many people think they can just eat
any old thing and they're not going
to suffer from it. But the laws of Nature
set up certain rules and regulations
that we have to follow if we want to
stay healthy."
                —Helen Conway, Nutritionist,
                Department of Health,
                City of New York

RECENTLY, Dr. Michael Lesser, a prominent psychiatrist specializing in nutritional medicine, made a revealing statement about nutrition and panic attacks. Here's what he said:

"Ninety-two percent of the patients that come to see me with symptoms such as anxiety, depression, fatigue, rapid heart palpitations, fearfulness, trembling, etc., had abnormalities in their blood sugar tests when I administered a five- or six-hour fasting glucose tolerance test to them.

"This has led me to draw the conclusion that a blood sugar abnormality is a physiological correlate of the neurotic symptoms. And that if a person is exhibiting symptoms of mental distress of a neurotic character, then it behooves the physician to look into their blood sugar, because very often they'll find there is a blood sugar abnormality. In fact, I find it practically to be the rule. And it may be that the quickest way to treat that person is to deal with that blood sugar abnormality. I'm not saying that the blood sugar abnormality causes the neurosis, nor am I saying that the neurosis causes the blood sugar abnormality. I prefer to think of the individual as a holistic creature, and the blood sugar pattern is simply a reflection of the disturbance in that individual throughout his whole system.

"However, I do think that in treating the blood sugar problem, you can often get a very quick response and improvement in that person's health and aid them with their symptoms. Sometimes you can get a complete clearing of their symptoms. Sometimes you can provide that individual with enough energy so that he can go ahead and tackle the important psychological difficulties that he has."

Diet and Resistance to Stress

If you own a dog or a cat, you've no doubt been asked by the vet what you're feeding your pet. Yet people are seldom asked by their doctors what their diet consists of. This never fails to astonish us. After all, even in ancient times many suspected a close link between diet and a person's health. "You are what you eat" is an old proverb. Scientific research and common sense observations have established such a link on numerous occasions. Here is just one example.

A recent study carried out through Johns Hopkins University involved young children in India—those who were well nourished and those who weren't. The malnourished children were not as adventurous. They were reluctant to explore their environment. They only wanted to stay close to Mother. They suffered from what the doctors called separation anxiety, which makes sense from Nature's point of view. To explore the environment takes a great expenditure of energy. But with limited resources, isn't it more important to conserve energy? After all, you can't afford to waste it. Your reluctance to leave your safe world and go out into the wide world may also relate to your nutritional condition.

But, you may say, how come I'm getting panic attacks

when many people eat worse than I do, and they don't get panic attacks at all?

That's a fair question. The point is we all have different tolerances for stress, and we're not all affected the same way. Some people get ulcers under stress. Some get panic attacks. The person suffering from panic attacks is already in a run-down condition. In order to pull himself out of this condition, his diet has to be more than just passable. An ordinary diet isn't good enough.

Moreover, those who suffer from recurrent panic attacks seem to have a higher inborn requirement for certain essential nutrients and for oxygen. Under stress, this simply becomes much more manifest. Why is this so? Because under stress, the metabolism quickens. The body has to make a greater effort at adjustment; more coping mechanisms are utilized. If a lot of energy is expended, more energy has to be generated. As we pointed out, this means an increased need for oxygen, glucose, and whatever else the cell needs.

When everything is going smoothly, when there's no special stress, you may be able to get by. But once there's added stress, there may be a problem. It's like a bridge: when there's only foot traffic, any old bridge will do. But when heavy trucks and cars have to cross, that bridge better be made stronger.

The PASS Food Plan

It doesn't take that much time or effort to put wholesome food on your table. In the long run, it's much more economical, too.

The food plan that follows gives you general information to make a good start.

These eight easy steps can put you on the road to recovery. Please check with your doctor, though, before you begin. He'll probably be delighted to give you a green light to go ahead. However, if you're on medication such as the MAO Inhibitors, your doctor will especially want to be consulted before you change your eating habits.

1. *Eat a varied, well-balanced diet based on the Basic Four food groups:*

   Protein Group: Fish, poultry, meat, eggs. Also nuts, peanut butter, legumes (beans, split peas, and so on). For additional high-quality protein (i.e., equal to animal protein), combine legumes with grains (rice with beans, pea soup with noodles, for example). Three servings daily.

   Milk Group: Milk, cheese, yogurt, buttermilk. (Milk, although in a group by itself, is also a protein food.) Two cups daily.

   Fruit and Vegetable Group: All vegetables, fresh fruits, salads: Eat a variety. Choose whole fruits rather than juice; avoid canned or frozen fruits packed in syrup. Cut way down the portion-size of fruits very high in sugars, such as bananas, figs, and raisins. Five to six servings daily.

   Bread Group: Whole grain bread, cereals, brown rice, and so on. Two to four servings daily.

   (The next time you're at the supermarket, make it a rule: Shop for the Basic Four *first*, then for whatever else you need.)
2. *Eliminate the simple sugars*.* Read food labels carefully: Corn syrup, sucrose, fructose, dextrose are all simple sugars and are found in many so-called convenience foods. Avoid alcohol, too.
3. *Spread out your meals so you have five or six mini-meals a day.* Eat something every three hours. When you go somewhere, it's best to bring your own food. Good food may not be readily available.
4. *Avoid caffeine.* Do not drink ordinary coffee, tea,

---

*Honey is a simple sugar, too, but it doesn't seem to elicit the insulin reaction the way sugar does. For this reason, it's acceptable in small amounts (in bread, for example).

chocolate, cola drinks. Find caffeine-free substitutes. There are many on the market today.

5. *Take a multiple vitamin/mineral supplement daily.* Also add (separately) a strong B-complex, the so-called nerve vitamin formula, and Vitamin C (about 1,000 mg., in time-release capsules). But remember: Vitamins are only food *supplements*; they are not food substitutes.

6. *Go easy on fats and salt.* (Remember, when you're reading labels, that sodium is another name for salt.)

7. *Remember the rule: A Protein Food with Every Meal.* Protein has staying power; it helps stave off hunger. But keep your protein portions small.

8. *Buy foods that have been tampered with as little as possible by the manufacturer.* Stay away from dietetic foods. If possible, buy organically grown and unsprayed fruits and vegetables. If a food label reads too much like a term paper in college chemistry, I'd put it back on the shelf.

A Quick Guide

Is there a quick and easy way to evaluate your diet?

We suggest you do the following. On a piece of paper, draw several of these diagrams:

PROTEIN	FRUITS & VEGETABLES
MILK	WHOLE GRAINS

For the next three days, using one diagram for each day, keep track of everything you eat, whether or not you follow the menu plan. Mark a line in the appropriate box. If you eat something that does not fit into a basic food group, put a check mark outside the diagram.

If, for example, you have this breakfast—oatmeal, egg, ½ orange, and ½ cup milk—record it as follows:

PROTEIN	FRUITS & VEGETABLES
1	½
MILK	WHOLE GRAINS
½	1

Notice the half-mark I made for the milk (½ cup) and for the orange. Continue recording the rest of your meals for that day; if you have five foods under a particular heading, write it like this: ⤚⤚⤙ . At the end of the day, if you're eating correctly you will have more lines in the two groups on the *right* side of the diagram.

A good diet is a high-fiber diet—that is, one high in fruits, vegetables, and grains. The foods on the left side, although contributing many other important nutrients, are also high in fat, and should therefore be eaten more sparingly.

Fresh Vegetable Soup

Who wouldn't enjoy a nice, hot bowl of soup—especially on a crisp, cool day? Soup is one of the easiest things to make. You don't need a complicated recipe. All you have to do is cut up vegetables, put them in water with a little seasoning, and let all the flavors simmer and blend together.

1. Start by frying an onion in a little oil—right in the soup pot—with a sprinkling of paprika. (The aroma alone will immediately establish your reputation as a terrific cook.)

2. Add water—and a package of dried soup mix

(such as split pea or minestrone) or beans that have been soaked overnight.

3. Add small quantities of any of these fresh vegetables:

carrots	peas
string beans	corn
potatoes, yams	mushrooms
tomatoes	leek
celery	spinach
beets/beet greens	okra

4. If you like, add a soup bone (although it really isn't necessary). To thicken the soup, add a "starch"—rice, uncooked oatmeal flakes, potatoes, or noodles, for example. (But be aware that some starches—like rice and barley—absorb a lot of water in cooking and can swell to several times their weight.)

5. For a beautiful, rich color, add tomato juice or a small can of tomato sauce. Spices? Try 2 bay leaves, 3 whole cloves, and a dash of pepper. You don't need to add salt.

6. It's not necessary to wait until the pot cools entirely before putting it in the fridge. (It's now been sterilized by boiling; prompt refrigeration won't let the bacteria multiply so fast—so you can keep the food longer.) If you're going to freeze some soup, fill small containers, but let them cool in the fridge before putting them in the freezer (to avoid defrosting nearby foods).

Do not overcook vegtebles; they lose vitamins in water. It's best to cook them in a vegetable steamer. You put this in the pot, so the vegetables sit on it and are cooked by the steam, not the water.

Festive Salad

A salad doesn't have to mean just lettuce-and-tomatoes. Put more color and enjoyment into it. Let it bring out the artist in you! Instead of pale iceberg lettuce, use deeper-green romaine lettuce (the richer the color, the more vitamins). Add other greens, too: raw spinach, parsley, broccoli, scallions, and more. For reds: Add tomatoes, radishes, cooked beets. Orange: Shredded or sliced carrots or orange wedges. Yellow: Kernels of cooked or canned corn—or crumbled hard-boiled egg yolks. Shredded purple cabbage adds a nice, bright touch. For color contrast, add raw mushrooms. It's a feast for the eyes as well!

Look for salad dressings on the market without added chemicals, or make a simple and delicious dressing by combining equal parts of oil and lemon with a pinch of crushed basil.

A Prototype Recipe

We've found that for many people the greatest obstacle to a good diet is food preparation. Sure, there are times when we might enjoy fussing in the kitchen and cooking. But few people like to do it every day, three times a day. (And we're asking you to eat even more than three times a day!) So it's very important to find quick and easy recipes. The store-brought convenience foods often contain too many chemical ingredients.

Here's something I (SAS) devised as a basic prototype recipe. It can be used over and over again, with a variety of ingredients, so you create countless new tastes and flavors. You don't get tired of this recipe so fast, and the more you use it, the easier it becomes to prepare.

Break 2 eggs in a large bowl, and beat them. (You can use only the egg whites, if you prefer.) Add 4 slices of crumbled whole wheat bread. Add a handful of raisins (for sweetness) and a slice of cheese cut into small pieces (for flavor). Now add 2 cups of 2 different vegetables. (If they're hard vegetables, steam them first, using a vegetable steamer.) Pour this mixture into a greased baking pan. Add more small pieces of cheese on top, and bake at 350°, until the cheese turns nice and brown.

Instead of the vegetables, you can use fruit; instead of the cheese, you can use spices; instead of the bread, you can use cooked rice (you can cook the rice beforehand), cooked or canned beans, potatoes, etc.

This is a high-fiber dish. It keeps well in the fridge, and you can grab a piece whenever hunger strikes. (I even like the vegetables cold.) When you make it with fruit and nuts, it's like cake, but it's a lot more nourishing.

K-Rations for Courage

When you first start going to those places you now fear, your emotions will be like those of a soldier going to the front lines. You will wonder: Will I come out of the "battle" okay? Will I make it? The high adrenaline output that can accompany such thoughts can be very draining.

Worry uses up a lot of energy. It can therefore rapidly deplete the normal supply of sugar in the blood. For that reason, it would be prudent to carry with you an emergency "K-ration." The food you take along should be something that can easily be absorbed into the bloodstream, yet provide some staying power. Moreover, it should also provide the vitamins and minerals your body will need in order to metabolize the sugar properly. So that rules out all junk food.

The best K-ration is a complex carbohydrate food plus a little bit of a protein food. Here are some examples:

Cheese/whole wheat crackers
Whole wheat crackers/ nuts/peach
Nuts/banana/cheese
Sliced meat/carrot sticks

Chicken/orange
Chicken/grapes
Hard-boiled egg/orange
Cheese/apple
Turkey/celery

Many of these can be brown-bagged and slipped into a purse.

Food Additives Considered to Be Safe

Food shopping used to be a lot simpler, but today many new chemicals are added to our food. Some of these chemicals have not been properly tested. Some have but are still on the market despite unfavorable reports.

Since additives cannot be avoided entirely, we're giving you a list of those chemicals that appear to be safe.*

Alginate; Propylene Glycol Alginate

Alpha Tocopherol

Ascorbic Acid; Erythorbic Acid

Beta Carotene

Calcium (or Sodium) Propionate

Calcium (or Sodium) Stearoyl Lactylate

Casein, Sodium Caseinate

Citric Acid; Sodium Citrate

EDTA

Ferrous Gluconate

Fumaric Acid

Gelatin

Glycerin (Glycerol)

Gums: Guar, Locust Bean, Arabic, Furcelleran, Ghatti, Karaya, Tragacanth

Hydrolyzed Vegetable Protein (HVP)

Lactic Acid

Lactose

Lecithin

Mannitol

Mono- and Diglycerides

Polysorbate 60

Sodium Benzoate

Sodium Carboxymethycellulose (CMC)

Sorbic Acid, Potassium Sorbate

Sorbitol

Starch; Modified Starch

Vanillin, Ethyl Vanillin

More Food for Thought

Try to buy organically grown fruits and vegetables that have not been sprayed with harmful insecticides. If you

*Center for Science in the Public Interest, 1501 16th St. NW, Washington D.C. 20036

live in a part of the country where such foods aren't available, an alternative is to grow your own. There are many helpful books available on home gardening.

In addition to the commonly known grains and cereals (wheat, rice, corn), also consider millet, buckwheat (not related to wheat), oats, and others. But buy the *whole* grains—those that have not been degerminated. If you enjoy a breakfast cereal, select one without BHT or BHA. Be wary of many so-called natural products. They may contain a lot of sugar. Make sure you read the label before you buy.

In many areas of the country, whole wheat bread is now standard fare at the supermarket. Remember: The package should say "whole wheat," not just "wheat." If at all possible, however, buy your breads at the health food store or local bakery. Their breads are usually minus the chemical additives of commercial bread.

Meat contains a high percentage of fat. The visible fat can be trimmed, but fat is also actually part of the meat-muscle itself. Remember: Fat has twice the calories of either protein or carbohydrates. Besides, hormones and antibiotics are often injected into cattle for greater growth. For these and other reasons, many doctors are now recommending to their patients to cut down on the consumption of red meat. If you *do* have meat, have a small portion and lots of vegetables—not the other way around.

Speaking of vegetables, the potato has a bad reputation that it doesn't deserve. It's not as fattening as many people believe, if you leave the butter off. Potatoes are a rich source of vitamins and minerals, and contain easily digestible protein.

Legumes (members of the bean family) have long been neglected in the typical American diet. But here's why they are important and should be included in your Food Plan:

1. Legumes are an excellent source of complex carbohydrates. They have consistently shown to cause a slow rather than a steep rise in blood sugar level. (Some researchers believe that's due to their high fiber content.)

2. Legumes are an important source of protein, especially when legumes and grains are eaten at about the same time.

If you've been avoiding beans because of gas discomfort, here's what you can do: Put the beans in water (one to five ratio of beans to water) and boil for ten minutes. Let the beans soak in this water overnight. Then drain this water and continue the recipe with fresh water. Some of the vitamins will be lost this way, but the protein will still be available.

Here's a good way to start building up a liking for a new food: Eat it when you're really hungry.

Whenever possible, eat the raw fruit rather than drink the juice. Fruit contains fructose (a simple sugar), but it also contains fiber and pulp, which the body breaks down slowly. Fruit juice, on the other hand, belongs more in the category of a refined food, since the fiber and pulp have been removed. If you're having juice, limit your serving to four ounces.

If you suspect a problem with food allergies, get a copy of *Dr. Berger's Immune Power Diet.* In it you'll find a "21-Day Elimination Plan" to help you discover which foods you might be allergic to. According to a number of researchers, severe food allergies can trigger panic attacks.

You may wonder if you can safely drink milk because of the connection between lactose and lactic acid and panic attacks. Don't worry. The lactose found in milk is processed in the digestive tract and has nothing to do with the lactic acid our own bodies make. So unless you happen to be allergic to milk, go ahead and drink it.

Is the new sweetener made from amino acids all right to use? We don't recommend it, since the chemicals used in its manufacture may possibly be carcinogenic. This product still has to be tested more adequately.

We're also wary of the newly proposed food-preservation method known as "food irradiation." (It involves zapping the food with high-energy, ionizing radiation.) Not only are some nutrients lost in some cases, but certain by-products of the radiation process itself have been found in the food. Although these by-products appear in very small quantities, they are unique to the radiation process and therefore of great concern to many scientists.

Vitamins

Should you or shouldn't you be taking vitamins?

We strongly suggest that you do. But with this caution: Vitamins are *not* food substitutes. They are only food supplements. Good nutrition must come from the diet, not from pills. You can't just eat anything you want to, and then take some pills to "make up for it." It doesn't work that way.

So why should you be taking vitamins? Your body has been exhausted and depleted because of the stress you've undergone, both the original stress that brought on the panic attacks in the first place and the daily stress you've been going through as a result of the repeated attacks. And you'll soon be going to new places or places you haven't been to in a long time. So you need all the help you can get.

Which vitamins should you take?

The vitamins stored in the body are A, E, D, and K. That means that if you take much, much more than you have to, it is possible that these vitamins might build up to a toxic level. The other vitamins are water-soluble, which means that they are not stored and any excess is washed out of the body.

The B-vitamins are part of a family known as the B-complex. They include:

B-1 (thiamine)
B-2 (riboflavin)
B-3 (niacinamide)
B-6 (pyrodoxine)
B-12
PABA
Folic acid
Choline

Inositol
Biotin
Pantothenic acid

Foods rich in B-complex include whole grains, organ meats, fish, poultry, fruits, vegetables (green, leafy vegetables—and other vegetables like broccoli and cauliflower), legumes, brewer's yeast, bran, and nuts.

The B-vitamins, long known to be essential for proper nerve function, are particularly deficient in the typical American diet, because they have been milled out of the flour. (In white enriched bread, almost two dozen nutrients have been removed, but only four put back.)

Carbohydrate metabolism requires B-vitamins. But sugar and white flour—the carbohydrates—the very foods that should be supplying these vitamins—don't! They use up B-vitamins without replenishing them.

Some of the B-vitamins—B-1, B-3, and B-6, are especially important in helping the body get rid of lactic acid. This is very significant, in view of what we said earlier about lactic acid and its relation to panic attacks. You should be taking higher doses of these particular vitamins. B-vitamins work best when taken together. So when you buy a B-complex formula, get one that includes all of the B-family. A moderately high dose would be around 50 mg.

Vitamins should always be taken with meals, not on an empty stomach.

Something to Think About

You've just finished a delicious meal. You put your napkin to your lips and murmur a few words of appreciation to the cook. As far as you're concerned, the meal is over.

But is it? As far as your body is concerned, the meal has just begun. Your body must now extract all the nutrients it needs to serve you better. Are you a good provider? Are you supplying the necessary raw materials?

We don't want you to feel that you must never, ever—under penalty of immediate panic attack—let even a small piece of chocolate or a smidgen of cake cross your lips. After all, in our society, good times and eating go together. We want you to live a good, normal life—which means going to parties, visiting friends, traveling, and so on. We know how tempting it is to see others eating all these forbidden foods. If you give in once in a while, the sky won't fall down. When your health returns and you're no longer in a run-down condition, an *occasional* taste (we don't mean binge) isn't going to harm you.

Altogether banishing such foods from your life ("I'll never, ever eat another piece of cake again as long as I live!") may only intensify your craving for them.

If you *do* have something sweet occasionally, have it *with* something, preferably a protein food. The impact of sugar or coffee is greater on an empty stomach, and blood sugar level rises much too quickly.

So please be easy on yourself and use common sense. An occasional looking-the-other-way is simply allowing yourself to be human. Just realize that your job is to feed and nourish *all* your body cells—not just your mouth. Think before you eat!

Caffeine

I (SAS) remember one of the first clients I had at PASS. He was a young surgical resident who was having a problem with panic attacks. He was often unable to operate because his hands were shaking so much. When I inquired about his diet, he mentioned that he had about twenty cups of coffee a day! I told him that was one of the reasons he was having panic attacks. His indignant reply was, "That can't be right. I've been drinking lots of coffee for years and it never bothered me before!" (He didn't stop to consider that he was evidently under much greater stress now.) "Besides," he went on, "there's nothing in the medical literature that says there's any connection between coffee and panic attacks."

Well, there is today. Dr. Thomas Udhe, a researcher at the National Institutes of Mental Health, did a study that demonstrated the detrimental effects of caffeine on panic-prone individuals. Calling caffeine the world's most widely used mood-altering drug, Dr. Udhe said, "Caffeine can cause panic attacks in panic disorder patients and, in sufficient quantities, can also trigger panic attacks in normal controls."

Caffeine is found not only in coffee, but also in tea, soft drinks and chocolate. It's also usually found in certain over-the-counter headache or cold remedies.

If you're in the habit now of taking large amounts of caffeine daily, you can help prevent withdrawal symptoms by tapering off *gradually*.

Alcohol and Panic Attacks

Sometimes a person will say, "I'm nervous, I need a drink." Often a person won't admit it, yet head for the bar just the same. But alcohol, like a high-sugar diet, does not solve the problem; in fact, it only makes it worse. It offers a quick fix, but there's hell to pay later.

The liver, in addition to being a storehouse for sugar, also has the ability to manufacture sugar from scratch (it uses the body's protein and fat to do this). This is done on an emergency basis after the body's own reserves of sugar have been used up. But alcohol blocks the liver's ability to do this. That means that if alcohol is taken on an empty stomach, without other food, the blood sugar level can drop dangerously low. And there's another factor, too: A too-high intake of alcohol depletes the body of certain nutrients—just as a high-sugar diet does.

We think many problem drinkers are really panic attack sufferers who are attempting to steady their nerves with alcohol. The catch is that it doesn't work.

Cigarettes and Panic Attackers

If you're a smoker, you've no doubt been equating cigarettes with relaxation. But scientific findings prove otherwise: Nicotine stimulates the sympathetic nervous system, and that's exactly what you don't want. The reason you feel better immediately after you inhale is because you've raised your blood sugar level. But don't forget, there's a rebound reaction later, just as there is with sugar.

A Swedish study (reported in the British medical journal, *Lancet*) showed a sharp rise in blood sugar level—as high as 35 percent—while smoking. The rapid fall that occurred later, said one researcher, "throws further light on the habit of chain-smoking . . . and the craving for another pick-me-up." When smokers were given cigarettes without the nicotine, the sharp rise and subsequent fall didn't occur.

You know, of course, without our telling you, how smoking cuts your oxygen intake.

Only a Part of the Pie

Remember, diet is only one facet of the recovery program. It is not the total picture. If you harbor all sorts of negative beliefs and see danger in every corner, you'll still have a problem with panic attacks. This constant stress and anxiety would soon wear out your alarm system. You have to change many things, not just one.

A client once told me that she sees the problem of panic attacks as a round circle, like a pie. Each part of the program (the 7 steps), represents a slice of the pie. So when you eat right, you take away a piece. When you change your attitude, that's another slice gone. When you exercise, another piece. Pretty soon nothing is left of the pie—and the panic attacks are gone!

CHAPTER 6

Step 2: Relaxation

"My presence will go with you, and I will give you rest."
—*Exodus* 33:14

Deep-Relaxation

AT A RECENT phobia conference, we saw a videotape of a young woman who had previously been homebound. The film showed her going on a bus trip for the first time. Throughout the entire trip, the young woman sat with clenched fists, wringing her hands over and over again. The cameraman kept zooming in on her hands. Had this young woman on the bus been taught to relax her voluntary muscles before and during the trip, she would have enjoyed her bus ride instead of sitting there in absolute agony.

Many people say they relax while watching TV or knitting. But this is not the relaxation we mean. We mean *deep* relaxation, where, for a period of twenty to thirty minutes a day, your body is so relaxed that it becomes as limp and loose as a rag doll.

It is physically impossible to be anxious (or to have a panic attack) and be relaxed at the same time. A muscle fiber is either all stretched out or tightly coiled. There's no in-between. It's like a light: It's either on or off. Muscle fibers work together in groups. As more and more muscle groups let go and uncoil, the tendency is for other muscle groups to join them—and the relaxation deepens. So by relaxing as many *voluntary* muscles as you can reach, you're relaxing the corresponding nerve cells, too. That's the whole idea: to get as many nerve cells as you can involved in the relaxation process *before* tension builds up.

There are two sets of nerves that connect the brain and the muscles. One set of nerves (sensory nerves) bring in sensations and information *from* the environment; another set of nerves (motor nerves) bring our messages *to* the environment. We touch, we move, we listen. Both sets of nerves are constantly being activated because we are always interacting with our environment. When one is deeply relaxed, nerve messages are dampened down. They're quieted. They rest. Thus, the relaxation period becomes a welcome respite to an overworked nervous system.

Relaxation is a skill. And, like any other skill, it can be learned. But it needs constant, daily practice. Your muscles somehow learn what relaxation feels like—by doing. They just get into a relaxed state more easily. It's like learning to dance: Somehow, after practicing many times, you just get out on the dance floor—and you do it. It just comes to you without thinking much about it.

What will daily relaxation practice do for you? It will tone down your general state of nervousness and reduce the irritability of the nervous system. Little things won't bother you as much. You won't be so overanxious all the time.

Deep Relaxation sessions not only relieve momentary tension and anxiety, their effects are cumulative, carrying over into real life situations as well. Each time you practice relaxation, you are training your muscles to know what complete relaxation feels like. So you're making it easier for them to remember the relaxed state. Thus, you can help head off a panic attack *before* it starts. You relax *before* the tension builds up—and overwhelms you.

So it's important that you set aside a definite time period of between twenty and thirty minutes every day to practice these exercises. Lock the door, take the phone off the hook, send the children outside to play. Do whatever you have to do to insure privacy, peace, and quiet. This is *your* block of time—for getting well!

Some people feel guilty when they take time for themselves. They see it as time taken away from their family. If this is how you feel, think of this: If you're sick, how can you take care of others? The best gift you can give your family is to be your best self. And this means you have to make the time to take care of your health—both your mental and your physical health.

Audio Relaxation

The best way to practice deep relaxation, we found, is by means of an audio-cassette tape. This embodies all the features of time-honored meditation—something to focus your attention on (a voice), a comfortable position, and so on—yet it doesn't require the initial training period that meditation does. You simply sit in a chair, close your eyes and listen to a soothing voice. As you listen, you create the images and scenes in your mind that the voice suggests. The more involved you become in this process, the better able you are to relax.

I (SAS) was first introduced to audio relaxation about twenty years ago by my dentist, Dr. Darwin Arkow, who once told me I was the most nervous patient he ever had. One day, I was in his office to have a filling, and he gave me a shot of Novocaine containing epinephrine (another name for adrenaline). I had a panic attack right there in the dental chair, and I refused to let him work on my tooth. The next time I came to the office, he tried gas. That didn't work either; I became nauseated. So he said to me, "Look, there's only one other thing I can try. It's a deep-relaxation method, but I'll need your full cooperation." At that point, I was eager to try anything. He talked and I listened. In a short time, I became so relaxed that when he started drilling, I felt no pain. I was absolutely amazed that the whole procedure was so comfortable and effective—and all he did was talk to me!

After that initial experience, I'd come to his office to get relaxed—never mind the cavities! And since I was so enthusiastic, he taped a relaxation session for me to keep. This, by the way, is what the PASS Group relaxation tape is based on. (There are a few relaxation tapes on the market today. If you would like to order ours, please see page 223 of this book.)

Probably the most important prerequisite for a good relaxation session is a passive, nonresistant attitude. This doesn't mean we want you to become a passive person. But during this half hour or so, we recommend that you let down your guard and become more receptive, more passive. Why? Because this is in the *opposite* direction of the fight-or-flight response. When the sympathetic nervous system has gained the upper hand, you need to elicit the opposite response in order to restore a balance.

During deep relaxation, the following beneficial physiological changes take place:

1. Your brain wave pattern subsides to the alpha state, a characteristic of the resting state.
2. Your oxygen consumption decreases.
3. The production of lactic acid drops.

The Deep-Relaxation Experience

What does deep relaxation feel like? It's a refreshing experience. When you open your eyes and stretch, it's as if you had a good night's peaceful sleep. Your body feels rested and your mind is clear and serene.

Here is a poem, sent in by one of our clients, Rachel Hill, that describes this feeling:

Meditation

A mantle of peace descends
And covers my shoulders with
Soft, white wings.

The impatience, the struggles,
The tightly-woven webs
Are all swept away.

A black velvet curtain falls
And stillness comes
Like the hushed moment at dawn;

A sweet, sweet quiet
Stills my limbs and tongue and eye;
The only sound is my own soft breath.

I love my world without clocks;
Each day I feel its stillness and peace,
Each day I am renewed.

Occasionally a client will report having difficulty with the idea of relaxing. It turns out that what they really fear is letting go. Because this is often equated with "losing control," and that's a scary thought to most panic attack sufferers.

May we suggest that you substitute the words, "getting floppy." It's a friendlier, even a more accurate, way of describing it. (This suggestion was given to us by Maralyn L. Teare, a clinical instructor of psychiatry at a medical center in Los Angeles.)

Relaxation Aids

There are a number of aids to relaxation. But please note: They are meant to *augment* the daily deep-relaxation sessions, not replace them.

Diaphragmatic Breathing

Did you know that when you take shallow breaths from the upper chest, you are activating the sympathetic nervous system? And that when you're under stress (i.e., when the sympathetic nervous system is already activated) your body switches *automatically* to upper chest breathing? They go hand in hand. Many nervous people are unaware that they're breathing from the upper chest and taking shallow breaths. If you breathe this way, you pave the way for hyperventilation because you're often not getting enough air and your body tries to compensate by breathing more.

On the other hand, diaphragmatic breathing—or abdominal breathing, as it's sometimes called—activates the parasympathetic nervous system, the calming one. It also brings in more oxygen to the lower lobes of the lungs—about 25 percent more, which can make a significant difference in the way you feel.

Fortunately, our breathing is partly under voluntary control. That means you can switch at will to diaphragmatic breathing whenever you're under stress.

How do you do diaphragmatic breathing? If your naval pushes out a bit as you inhale, you're doing it correctly. (Imagine a balloon in your stomach, and as you inhale, imagine the balloon filling with air.) Next time you look at a sleeping baby, observe how the baby breathes. Relaxed. Even. Watch his tummy push up and down rhythmically. That's what you have to emulate.

It's interesting to note that abdominal breathing does *not* come automatically (the way chest breathing does, under stress). You have to learn it. Or, rather, relearn it. Because this is the way we used to breathe when we were babies.

Slow, "Soft" Stretches

If you're more tense than usual before you begin the deep-relaxation session, or if you want to achieve a greater degree of relaxation, take five or ten minutes to prepare yourself with slow, physical movement.

Soft stretches stretch out the muscles and gently ease away tension. Dr. Edmund Jacobson, a Chicago physician who began his research in relaxation techniques back in the 1920s, noted that when you tense a muscle, hold the tension for some seconds, and then let go, the subsequent relaxation of the muscle is greater than if you hadn't tensed the muscle at all.

The effect is very much akin to that of stylized Chinese exercise, tai chi chuan, done every morning in Chinese town squares by young and old alike. Because when you do the exercises very slowly, you are holding the tension for several seconds.

You can simply turn on the radio, find some soft music, and dance freestyle. Raise your hands above your head often as you dance; turn from side to side often, raise your legs high. Do a variety of body movements, but very slowly.

Or you can do your regular calesthenic exercises (that you normally do every day) in very slow motion.

Eye Relaxation Exercises

Did you know that the eyes are considered an extension of the brain? And that if the eyes are completely relaxed, it's easier for the whole body to become relaxed too?

Here are some eye exercises that you can do from time to time during the day. One advantage of these exercises is that you can do them almost anywhere, even at work.

Palming: Place your elbows on a table. Cup both hands and put them over your eyes so that your face rests in the palms of your hands. Don't touch your eyes at all; merely hold the bony structure around your eyes. Sit this way for a few moments, thinking of pleasant scenes of nature or places you'd like to visit.

Eye-Writing: You can sit or lie down. Close your eyes. Simply "draw" some figure 8's, circles, letters of the alphabet, etc., with your eyes.

Near Vision/Far Vision: Whenever you read a lot or do close work, rest your eyes from time to time by looking for a few moments at distant objects.

The QR

What is the QR? It stands for Quieting Reflex. It's a technique that was developed by Charles F. Stroebel, M.D., a Hartford, Connecticut, neurologist/psychiatrist. The QR is simple to do—it takes only six seconds, but it is remarkably effective in relieving tension*:

*Reprinted by permission. *QR: The Quieting Reflex* by Charles F. Stroebel, M.D., Berkley Publishing, 1983.

Stop or s-l-o-w down (sit, if you wish).

2. *Relax your facial muscles* by doing the following:
   a. Smile inwardly.
   b. Imagine the smile coming across your face and spreading up towards your eyes. (Make sure your teeth and jaw are unclenched.)
   c. Say to yourself: "My eyes are twinkling and sparkling."

3. *Take a deep abdominal breath.*
   a. Imagine you are inhaling through holes in the bottoms of your feet, up through your legs, and into your stomach.
   b. Feel the upward flow of warmth and "heaviness."

4. *As you exhale slowly:*
   a. Imagine the air flowing back down through holes in your feet, taking all the tension along with it.
   b. At the same time, let your jaw, tongue and shoulders go limp.

(Repeat once more)

You're probably wondering: How can such a simple technique be so helpful? Here's the rationale behind it:

1. The sentry is constantly receiving messages of the state of tension (or relaxation) of all the muscles in the body. (This is without our conscious awareness.) If the sentry receives messages that the muscles are generally in a relaxed state, the sentry relaxes too. Therefore, when you slow down (and don't rush), you're encouraging your over-alert sentry to relax too.

2. Notice that the exercise involves many muscles in the facial area. Remember, muscles and nerves are connected. The corresponding nerve cells of the facial muscles occupy a large part of the brain. For example, there are more nerve bundles for your tongue than, say, for a much larger area in your back. Therefore, what the facial muscles do carries a lot of weight, so to speak. When the facial muscles relax, a great number of nerve bundles in the brain relax too.

As you will soon see, you can help your body relax through the use of appropriate imagery. The cells can't tell the difference between what's real and what isn't. If you imagine relief in the form of warmth and comfort, your muscle cells respond and let go.

3. The deep breathing helps provide more oxygen to the brain, and it also helps to relax the chest muscles. When the muscles in your legs relax, they stop pressing against the blood vessels there, so more blood is able to get through. This makes your legs feel stronger, more sturdy. The jaws are generally clenched during stress; the shoulder muscles are tight and hunched up (ready for fight or flight). Therefore, if you relax those muscles consciously, it conveys this message to the sentry and helps counteract any stress buildup.

4. Powerful imaginery is evoked when you "see" all the tension leaving your body (what a relief *that* is!).

So, whenever you begin to feel tense or hurried, that should be a signal for you to immediately switch gears and do the QR. You can do it 100, 200 times a day; the more you practice, the better, because it will reinforce the QR as a response to tension, and after a while the response will become automatic. In other words, a reflex action.

Do you see what a valuable tool this can be? You can do the QR anywhere, in almost any situation. And all it takes is a moment of your time. (Even if you do it 100 times, it's still only ten minutes a day.)

First Aid Treatment for Panic Attacks

It's important to learn how to prevent a panic attack, but you must also learn how to deal with a panic attack, if you have to. When you know you have a backup system, when you know you can do something to help yourself, it gives you greater assurance.

Remember the scene we described at the beginning of this chapter—the young woman on the bus? As I watched the film, it reminded me of the way they used to depict childbirth scenes in movies about the olden days. The mother would grab and hang on to a cloth that was tied to the bedpost whenever a contraction came. Contrast this with the natural childbirth method now proposed by Dr. Grantly Dick-Read of England (*Childbirth Without Fear*). It is precisely during the contraction that the mother is taught to relax and let go, in order to allow the womb to open up. Allowing the contraction to come in a wave—without resistance or interference—greatly diminishes, and in many cases even eliminates the pain. (Pain and fear are very similar. Both involve tense muscles; naturally, the tenser the muscle, the worse the pain—or the fear.)

Similarly, it's at the moment of panic that you have to train yourself to respond by letting go, by getting floppy. The natural tendency is to tense up even more. But in doing that, you're actually setting yourself up for more tension. The best advice we can give you is this:

1. Slow down, stop. (Don't run away.) Sit down, if possible. Take two deep abdominal breaths, hold for a count of four, and exhale slowly.
2. Get floppy. Feel your body's "heaviness." Feel gravity pulling you down.
3. Think health. While waiting for the storm to subside, remind yourself what the doctor said—how healthy and strong you really are.

Later, when it's all over, ask yourself: How did that come on? Was it more mind or body? Did I scare myself with all those what-ifs again? Have I been pushing myself too hard lately and neglecting my health? When was the last time I ate, and what did I eat?

CHAPTER 7

Step 3: Exercise

"Exercise is like taking a Valium."
—*Jane Brody,*
science editor of
The New York Times

WHY IS EXERCISE so soothing?

Pam Colari, a former dancer and physical education instructor, explains why in the following interview:

PAM: Exercise actually reduces stress. You see, stress is a form of muscle tension. When you have all the stress built up in your body, it's like a wild animal who's been angered. You're ready to pounce. And what you want to do is to reduce all this muscle tension. If you exercise, it's going to be a release from all this tension that's built up in the muscles.

We have many secretaries that come into this spa, and it's really amazing that when they come in—when we get the crew that comes in right after work—like I'm afraid to talk to half of these people. They all look so mean and so angry.! So I just give them a quick hello. But when they leave, it's like, you know, "Have a nice evening"—and they feel wonderful!

SHIRLEY: This is so true. I used to go to a gym on my lunch hour. My boss was a wonderful guy, really, but sometimes he'd frazzle my nerves. I used to go to a gym so I could have an exercise break, and I'd come back to the office feeling so wonderful, so relaxed. And I'd also feel so kindly toward my boss, I'd forget how he was in the morning!

PAM: Let me add this also: When people get this stiff neck in the back, when they say, "Oh, I'm so tense, I need a massage," what happens is that the muscles have just tightened up into little balls. And by working that out, you're going to feel so much better. You can get a headache from muscle tension, too, from tightening up the muscles of the neck.

SHIRLEY: Yes, that can be a pain in the neck . . . ! Tell me, what about older women? Many people believe that because they haven't exercised regularly or they exercised and stopped that maybe it's too late for them to start now.

PAM: It's never too late. The human body is an amazing organism. You can start exercising at any time. The one important thing to keep in mind is that you should start slowly if you haven't exercised in a long time. And you should have a checkup from your doctor because there may be things you should know about. If you start exercising slowly, you'll be able to build up your body to what it should be. Then you just keep it up.

SHIRLEY: Speaking about age, it's interesting that many astronauts are in their forties—some of them in the late forties. And here these people were picked just because they were in top physical shape! So when women say to me, at age forty, I can't exercise, I'm over the hill, I have to laugh.

PAM: Sure, it's true. The body can be taught how to do almost anything. It's very trainable.

On a recent TV show we saw a sixty-eight-year-old woman who had taken up karate a few years ago to relieve arthritis and then went on to earn a black belt, the highest award in karate! She delighted the audience by breaking wooden boards with swift kicks—and she's only four eleven and weighs about one hundred pounds.

If such a miraculous turn-about was possible for this woman, why not for you?

Aerobic Exercises

Aerobic exercise trains your body to deliver oxygen more efficiently. As your body attempts to adjust to the tough demands of these exercises, your oxygen-delivery system becomes stronger.

Here are some examples of aerobic exercises:

Swimming	Dancing (if moving arms
Walking/running/walking	and legs)
Brisk walking	Jogging
Running in place	Jumping rope
Bike riding	Calisthenics (if continuous)
Rowing	

There are many other exercises that help strengthen and develop the outside muscles of the body—weightlifting and yoga are two examples. But these are not aerobic. They don't teach the body to process oxygen because they don't continue long enough and they don't give the heart and lungs a good enough workout.

In order to qualify as aerobic, an exercise must be done nonstop for at least twelve minutes. It must also raise the pulse rate to approach—but not exceed—about 80 percent of your maximum heart rate.

How do you know what your maximum heart rate is?

The maximum heart rate is based not on how physically fit you are (as you might suppose), but on your age. So the table below has already been worked out for you:

Age	Six-Second Interval
16–20	16
21–35	15
36–50	14
51–55	13
56–65	12
66 +	11

Note that you take your pulse for six seconds.
Since it's difficult to measure your pulse while exercis-

ing, do it immediately following the exercise. Remember, your pulse rate declines as soon as you stop exercising, and the better condition you're in, the sooner it goes down.

The wrist pulse is often hard to find, so check your carotid artery instead. Just place two fingers of one hand about two inches away (to the right or left) from your Adam's apple. You needn't check your pulse rate each and every time you exercise—only at the beginning— until you get the hang of it.

Many people have asked this question: If you have your doctor's permission to exercise but you haven't exercised for some time, do you ease into an exercise program gradually? Do you start, say, with three minutes of exercise and build up to twelve minutes?

The answer is, it's not necessary. You can start immediately with the twelve minutes. The key, of course, is the pulse monitoring. A person who is very much out of condition certainly won't be able to do much without getting his pulse rate way up. On the other hand, a person who is in excellent physical shape might have to jog at a fast pace to reach the same heart rate. So the kind of exercise will be different for each person, depending on the condition they're in.

However, if you feel uncomfortable about pulse checking and the twelve minutes of exercise at first (and many do), you can build up the time gradually. Ultimately, aim for a half-hour exercise period a day, which should also include nonaerobic exercise.

There's a new kind of aerobic exercise called "low impact aerobics (LIA)." The basic idea is to keep one foot on the floor at all times while doing the calesthenics in order to put less strain on the joints. This would probably be a more suitable exercise for an older person or one who is very overweight.

"But It Makes My Heart Beat Faster!"

Many people who suffer from panic attacks feel uncomfortable about exercising. They're worried that if they exercise, it will make their rapid heartbeat worse. If this is your concern, you should be aware that a progressively difficult program of exercise—in the long run—will slow down—*not* increase—the heart rate. This happens automatically, through training. So you needn't fear that exercise will make your heartbeat even faster. It won't. It will do the opposite. (Did you know that the average person's resting pulse rate is about seventy beats per minute—while a trained runner's might be only forty?)

Of course, if you're overdoing aerobic exercise—if you work too hard and go into oxygen debt—then, obviously, you're defeating your own purpose. We never recommend too-strenuous exercise. In fact, exercise can trigger the panic attacks, if you overdo. One of our clients was a marathon runner. He ran an average of ten miles a day—and sometimes a lot more. When he cut his practice run down to three miles a day (and improved his diet, too, I might add), the panic attacks stopped.

Exercise, remember, is a stress to the body. Scientists use running as a means of applying stress to laboratory animals when they want to study its effects. They have the animals run a treadmill. But when running is done in moderation, it's a mild stress—and therefore beneficial to the body. Why? Because in adapting itself to meet that stress, the body is encouraged to work better, to perform more effectively.

Why You Should do a Variety of Exercises

Twelve minutes on aerobics and twenty on yoga, calisthenics, stretching exercises, or weightlifting—gives you a well-rounded program that works all your muscles.

Why is this important?

Your muscles work in teams. One set of muscles pulls one way—the opposing muscles pull the other way. So if you do only one kind of exercise, you develop only one member of the muscle team. But by doing a variety of exercises, you get a better-balanced muscle workout—and a nicer-looking body.

Another reason for doing a variety of exercises is that you don't want it to get boring. It's absolutely vital for good health. So make it fun!

Easy Aerobics

Here's an aerobic exercise that appeals to many people because it's so simple. You don't need complicated or costly equipment. You can watch TV or listen to the radio at the same time.

Get a box that's sturdy enough to stand on. Just step on the box; step down; on and off, on and off. If you're out of condition, choose a small box (about six inches high); otherwise, you can use a milk box or a chair. You have to change feet, though, so you don't use the same foot to go up all the time. So—it's right step up, left step up; right step down, left step down; step-step-step. Then: left step up, right step up, and so on. If you have small children, they can join you in this exercise, on their own little boxes.

"But I'm Too Tired to Exercise"

Very often someone will say, "I know I should be exercising, but I'm just too tired; I have no strength." They reason: If I exercise, I'll only become more tired. But it's just not so. It actually works the opposite way: The more you ask of your body (well, within reason . . .), the more it delivers. A good physical workout will energize you and revive you—because you'll be using your body in an intelligent, healthful way.

Naturally, you mustn't overdo. "Never bite off more than you can chew!" applies to exercise as well as to other areas of life. But you'll notice that as you continue to exercise, as you get stronger, your muscles will just want to do more. You don't have to push yourself; this comes by itself as you train every day.

A Word About Jogging

We often see joggers running alongside cars even on the busiest streets and highways, and can't help wondering. These people are presumably doing this exercise for health reasons, yet they're right next to cars that are continually spewing toxic exhaust fumes. When a person does aerobic exercise on a regular basis, his body adapts itself to the demands: The passages to the lungs expand to take in more air. All this is good; this is why exercise is so beneficial. But if you're jogging along a busy street, aren't you taking in a lot more polluted air? (The people in the cars are sitting, so their lungs are not working as hard. They're also encased in their own air space, so they're getting less outside pollution.) If you're going to jog, it should only be done in areas away from cars and buses.

What About Lactic Acid Buildup?

But, you may ask, when you exercise, you're contracting muscle—so doesn't that produce more lactic acid?

The answer is yes, it does. But if you've been exercising aerobically on a regular basis, you've also increased your body's capacity to remove lactic acid. There's a greater oxygen exchange going on now. More blood is being brought to various areas of the body by the exercise itself. More blood brings in more oxygen and carries away the waste. So you're actually neutralizing the lactic acid.

Getting Rid of Anger

Exercise can be put to other uses besides cardiovascular training. It can be used as a muscle relaxant. And it can be used to diffuse anger and frustration.

When you're angry, your hormones scream for action. Yet civilization (or simple, common decency!) often prevents you from acting. So, let your imagination come to the rescue: Take a pillow and give it the old one-two. Remember—your hormones can't tell the difference between real and not-real. When your mind-imagery shouts, "Take THAT (POW!), you old witch!"—it feels as if it's actually happening. But the blessing is that you needn't feel guilty afterward, because you haven't done anything wrong. You haven't harmed anyone. And, besides, it's just *your* secret. Later, when you're all cooled off, you might talk to that person about why you were angry, if you think it will serve a useful purpose.

Some Commonsense Precautions

- Make sure you check with your doctor before beginning any exercise program.
- Don't begin an exercise program if you are just recovering from a cold, flu, or other illness. When you resume exercises again, do so gradually.
- Never overdo! Pace yourself. Work at a speed that feels comfortable for you. "Train; don't strain."
- Always begin an exercise session with a warm-up (a slow-motion routine) to wake up your body gradually.

CHAPTER 8

Step 4: Attitude

"It is part of the cure to wish to be
cured."

—Seneca

Wanting to Be in Control

PEOPLE ARE always saying, "I want to be in control." But
what does it mean? What does it mean to you?

If it means feeling well, feeling "on top of the world,"
being pleased and satisfied with yourself—that's one thing.
But to many people it means something else. They want
to see themselves doing the right thing on each and every
occasion—whether it's speaking before a group or being
sociable at a party. They want to eliminate any shred of
nervousness or indecision or vulnerability. They want to
appear "cool." These people are often deathly afraid of
losing control. The solution, they think, is to "get a tight
grip" on themselves or to "get hold" of themselves. They
want to whip their nervous systems into instant obedi-
ence. And they want to be able to diminish the panic
attacks through brute strength or sheer willpower.

But, as you've no doubt discovered, this can't be done.
In many ways, the emotional brain behaves like a balky
two-year-old child. Give it a direct command—and it
immediately says no and does the opposite. The more
you force and push and strain, the more stubborn the
mind becomes.

How do you handle a contrary autonomic nervous
system? If brute strength and direct force won't work,
what will?

Well, why not try the same strategy that you might try
with that stubborn two-year-old? It wants to do the opposite? Fine. Then let it.

Let's take as an example an act that's controlled by the autonomic nervous system: sleep. Say you're trying to get to sleep because you have an important meeting in the morning and you want to be fresh and alert. So you tell yourself, "Sleep, dammit, sleep!" Can you fall asleep easily? No, not with *that* tone of voice. But if you tell yourself, "It's okay—so what if I miss a night's sleep? Nothing'll happen. I'm even gonna pretend the alarm just went off and I've got to get up soon . . ." If you say this instead, chances are you'll soon fall asleep. And even if you don't sleep a whole night you'll still get a good night's rest and feel refreshed in the morning. This strategy always works for me (SAS). Even if I don't sleep all night, I still feel fine in the morning because I relaxed and just thought of pleasant things.

I used to have another habit governed by the autonomic nervous system—this one was making an ugly facial grimace whenever I was under stress. I tried to stop, but couldn't. All my efforts to stop only made it worse. Then I tried the *opposite* approach—I tried to make myself do it. I soon dropped the habit.

One of our clients had difficulty swallowing—and, naturally, she became fearful about the possibility of choking. Three doctors assured her there was no physical abnormality in her throat, yet the difficulty persisted. I explained to her how the autonomic nervous system works, and suggested that she just chew her food and try *not* to swallow. She did that—and, of course, the food went down easily.

Another client had this problem: She would blush whenever she went out in public. To her, this was agonizingly painful, and she practically became a recluse as a result. Again, I explained the paradoxical way the autonomic nervous sytem works, and how forcing herself *not* to blush would actually bring it on! I advised her to *force* herself to blush instead. She didn't believe me but decided to give it a try, anyhow. The next time I spoke to her, she reported with great surprise that for the first time in years, she didn't blush in the presence of other people. "I tried very hard to blush," she said, "but couldn't!"

One man I remember decided to test this theory in what I thought was a rather dramatic way. He drove at night to a certain street that he hadn't been to in years because of his fear of having a panic attack there. He got out of the car and yelled, "OK, panic attack, here I am. Come and get me!" And you know what happened? Nothing!

There's a school of psychiatry, known as logotherapy, which incorporates as one of its basic tenets this curious phenomenon about the autonomic nervous system. The founder of logotherapy, Dr. Viktor Frankl, calls it the "Principle of Paradoxical Intention." But what he does is carry this idea one step further. He instructs his patients to engage in a self-dialogue and *deliberately exaggerate the nervous symptom to the point of absurdity*. For example, if a person is bothered by moist palms due to nervousness, he might say, "My hands are sweaty? Good! I'll show 'em sweaty! I'm gonna fill three buckets full and line 'em up so everyone'll see what a great sweater I am! They'll put my name in the Guinness Book of World Records!" Or: "Am I starting to get 'rubbery' legs again? Fine! I'm gonna make 'em even more rubbery. My legs'll bounce and I'll start jumpin' around like a kangaroo!"

The purpose of exaggerating the symptoms until they appear ludicrous is to inject a little humor into the situation. We all know that "laughter is the best medicine." Once you can smile or laugh and not take yourself so seriously, your nervousness vanishes.

Hans O. Gerz, M.D., a Connecticut psychiatrist who uses this method with his patients, says, "If I'm seeing a patient who's afraid of passing out, for example, I ask the patient to get up and try to pass out right here in my office. To evoke humor in the patient, I might say, 'Come on, let's have it. Let's pass out all over the place. Show me what a wonderful passer-out you are.' So the patient tries to pass out—and when he finds he can't, he starts to laugh."

So that's one way of exerting control over the autonomic nervous system: Knowing that it cannot be pushed—

and refraining from pushing it and even making it do the opposite (with humor!).

But there's another way, too. Let me tell you a little story.

There was a famous Russian scientist by the name of Aleksandr Luria, who was well known for his work on brain function. His special area of interest was the autonomic nervous system, and he became involved in the study of a man who could apparently control his autonomic nervous system at will. This man was able to voluntarily increase or decrease his heart rate, dilate or constrict his pupils, and so on. Professor Luria wondered: How did this man do it? How could he perform these amazing feats that nobody else could do?

It turned out that the man himself had once stumbled upon a method, which he had perfected through practice. What he would do was invent an appropriate "picture story" to match the effect he wanted to create. For instance, if he wanted to speed up his heart rate, he would imagine he was at a railroad station, trying to catch a train that was just pulling out of the station. He saw himself armed with luggage, running, running, huffing and puffing—and his heart rate would go up. When he wanted to slow down, he'd just imagine himself lying comfortably in bed, dozing off, ready to fall asleep. If he wanted to decrease the size of his pupils, he'd imagine a very strong light shining in his eyes, and so on.

This man seemed to be willfully regulating his autonomic nervous system. But, as you can see, he didn't do so directly, either. He didn't defy any natural laws. He merely used his imagination as a tool to prod his autonomic nervous system to react in a way that he wanted it to react.

So you see, you *do* have control over the panic attacks, although not in a direct, aggressive way.

Listening to Your Courageous Self

Among our many Selves, we have a dependent, timid Self—and a bold, courageous Self. The timid Self is always crying, "Wh-who me? Oh, no, I c-c-can't," and the bold Self stands up straight, looks 'em in the eye, and declares, "Oh, yes, I can"; "I will; I want to!" Sometimes one voice takes over, sometimes the other. Nobody can be brave all the time—or even most of the time.

But there's a paradox here (how those paradoxes keep cropping up!) and it's this: How that small, timid, dependent Self can have such a strong, loud voice—to drown out that courageous voice! And the courageous voice inside—that foundation of strength—often speaks to us in such a low, meek, soft voice—almost a whisper. (Many times the voice is so low, it can hardly be heard.)

So, your job—if you want to become more courageous—is to strengthen your bold, daring Self. How? By listening for its voice: by encouraging it; by bringing it out more—just as you would encourage a very young, bashful child. (You don't yell at it or criticize or condemn it.) When you *do* hear that little voice, you praise it, you congratulate it!

Obviously, you haven't done all this before. What happened was that you blamed yourself when you lacked the courage to do something. Instead of listening for that inner, daring voice, you became angry at yourself because it didn't speak out loud enough to suit you. But you were the one who criticized it and put it down—who else?

So now you have to allow that courageous voice inside to speak up more clearly, in order to create a proper balance. Just as the parasympathetic nervous system must now be strengthened in order to become equal to the now-dominant sympathetic nervous system, so must the inner courageous voice be strengthened until it can speak just as loudly as the timid voice is speaking now.

Does it sound like a difficult task? It needn't be. In fact, it can be a great, exhilarating experience—if you let it. Each time you do something that you really wanted to do but held back before, because you were afraid—each time you do it anyhow, you'll find it satisfies you on some deep, inner level. Because you've met the challenge—and that's the important thing.

Young animals, including children, seem to be—by nature—endowed with this gift of wanting to do and learn and try—in spite of fear. No—not in spite. Because of fear. Author Richard Bach describes this feeling accurately and with great poignancy:

> Remember the challenge of the high board at the swimming pool? After days of looking up at it, you finally climbed the wet steps to the platform. From there it was higher than ever. But there were only two ways down: the steps to defeat—or the dive to victory. You stood on the edge, shivering in the hot sun, deathly afraid. At last, you leaned too far forward. It was too late for retreat, and you dived off the edge. Remember? The high board was conquered in that instant—and you spent the rest of the day climbing steps and diving down.
>
> Climbing a thousand high boards, we live. In a thousand dives, demolishing fear, we turn into human beings.

If we let the "I c-c-can't" voice gain the upper hand, if we give in to it every time it screams, how are we ever going to do anything new?

Doing something new often requires a new way of looking at things. Many people have a fear of contradiction; they fear being inconsistent. So they become stuck in a mold and they can't get out. But what's so terrible about appearing inconsistent? (I remember, at a discussion-group meeting, a man made a statement and a little later, he said the exact opposite. Another man pointed this out to him, accusing him of being inconsistent. And he replied, "So? Where is it written that a human being must be consistent?")

One creative solution to the problem of contradiction is to accept and assimilate both parts—one and the other. In this case, it means accepting the dependent, timid Self as well as the bold, courageous Self. It's important that you make friends with that dependent self—and not dislike it or reject it (as some of you may want to do), but treat it as a part of your Self, with compassion and understanding. Only then will the strong, more mature part of yourself be able to shine through. (And isn't that another paradox?)

Of course, you don't have to take all this literally—this notion of many Selves residing inside, like little Russian dolls, one within the other. It's just a handy way of looking at this important issue of the two sides of ourselves—the one that wants to hold back and the one that wants to move forward. It's easier to do something about the problem if we view it, in a fanciful way, as two separate voices, each attempting to take over, because then the answer becomes simple: Make that courageous voice louder. Tune up the volume.

We think it would be helpful for you to keep a written record of your inner dialogue—say, for several days or a week. Simply divide a sheet of paper into two columns (as shown)—and in the left-hand column, write down what your dependent, timid self says. Then let your independent, courageous self answer it. To give you an example, here's what one client wrote:

My timid, fearful, dependent Self says:	*My bold, courageous, daring Self answers:*
"It's 6 A.M. already. Time to get up. Why do I feel so dizzy? Look at how I look in the mirror! I must be sick!"	"I better get to bed earlier tonight, instead of watching that late-night movie. Of course I feel dizzy. It's been hours since I've eaten anything. As soon as I've had breakfast, I'll feel much better."
"Why do I feel so lousy? I feel so uneasy. What's that funny feeling in my stomach? I'm feeling horrible and now my head is also beginning to feel funny."	"So what if I feel a little off today. No one feels great every day of the week. I'm not making the situation any better by tuning into myself so much. Stop being so introspective, and concentrate on something else. Maybe do some exercises and concentrate on my body in a more constructive way."

"I have to go out and do some errands, but I don't think I can. I feel so anxious. It's almost as if I can't move. Maybe I should stay home and wait until this goes away."

"The feelings will go away, but they'll come back when you decide to go out again! Of course you feel anxious. This is still relatively new for you. Instead of thinking of being anxious, do what they say at PASS, and substitute the word excited. That doesn't sound bad at all."

"What a place to get a panic attack—at a PTA meeting. Oh, I feel so awful and I want to leave. I have to get out of here!"

"Stop! Take two deep, slow breaths and make your body heavy. The feeling will pass. The meeting began to get boring, and you started looking inward. Your mind brought this on, so wait and it will pass."

Notice how she gives equal time to both sides (most people, when they first start keeping accounts, give more weight to the left side of the column). This client is now fully recovered and doing just great!

Avoid Negative Chain Reactions

Herman Wouk, the novelist, once wrote in one of his books, "Viewpoint is everything." It may not be everything—but it's very, very important.

Let's pretend we're both sitting in a living room, facing each other. Between us is a low table with a vase of flowers on it. We both look at the flowers, but we each see a different view because we're looking at it from a different perspective. Your view is real—but my view is just as valid as yours. So all I'm asking you to do is to come around to my side of the table and take another look. Step aside for a moment—and try to change the way you habitually view things. Get a new attitude. What does that mean? A new attitude means seeing truth in a different way.

And when you try to look at something from a different angle, a whole new train of thought emerges. Because one thought always leads to another. So you can either escalate the panicky feelings (by a train of thought) or deescalate it.

Let's say you're by yourself and you start to think, "I'm by myself." You can turn this sentence in a decidedly negative direction by continuing this way: "I'm all alone. Oh, my gosh, that means if I get a panic attack, nobody will be able to help me. Oh, that would be terrible. I'd be lying there, who-knows-how-long. I'd go crazy. I wouldn't be able to help myself. I wouldn't know what to do. I must have someone with me. Oh, help me, someone, anyone . . . !"

But a different chain of thought might be: "I'm by myself—I'm on my own. But I don't have to worry too much about a panic attack. Because if it comes, I know what to do. I can review the PASS-Group book. Others have made it—why can't I? It's really pleasant to be by myself—with no one to bother me. Maybe I'll finish that project I started. Hey, this is going to be fun." See what I mean?

Here's another example: "I'm five miles from home." One train of thought can run: "Oh, I've gone too far this time—Now there's nobody around who knows me—I'm all alone—nobody cares what happens to me—what if I get a panic attack here?" (You can guess what happens next.)

But, starting from the same premise, "I'm five miles from home," it can also run like this: "How wonderful that I can travel now—that I'm not bedridden or helpless—that I can enjoy the sunshine today—that I can make my life more interesting now—oh, look at this, I've never seen that before—what an interesting color on that leaf—what a lovely world the good Lord made—and this is all my world, too! It's so good to be alive," etc.

Here are a few more examples: Say, a person fails at something: "I've failed—that's terrible—that means I'm no good—now people won't like me anymore—nobody will care for me—I'll be all alone," etc., etc. Or, he could say: "I've failed. Well, you can't win 'em all . . . But I wonder what went wrong—Why didn't this thing succeed? Was it because of such-and-such? Probably. Or maybe it was because I did such-and-such. Yes, that's it—let's see—oh, I know what I'll try next time—yes, I think that'll work out much better—there; that's settled—yes, I'm sure that'll do the trick—great. Boy, I can hardly wait to try it out next time and see what happens," etc. (Do you see the hopeful note?)

Say a person has a panic attack. He says to himself: "Oh, my goodness, this terrible feeling came over me just now. It must mean I'm going crazy!! Oh, my goodness! Or maybe it's my heart— maybe I'm having a heart attack right now?! Oh, they're gonna have to call an ambulance now . . . ! And I'm all alone here . . . what'll I do?? Oh, this is terrible, terrible!! I think I'll start screaming in a minute . . . Oh, I can't stand it! I'm gonna lose control, I know it! I know it! Oh, what'll I do—? I'm never going to come here again!" etc.

But he can say this instead: "Wow, that left me shaky . . . I wonder what that was all about? Maybe it's trying to tell me something . . . I know I was under too much of a strain lately . . . I was trying to do too much . . . and I also let myself get run-down . . . that's probably what it was . . . I'm just going to have to start taking better care of myself . . . I'm going to eat right, go to sleep earlier from now on . . . get some more rest because of the hours I've been keeping lately . . . and I'll see what happens . . ."

Watch Your Language!

One of the things people frequently do when they say negative things to themselves is use the word "never." ("I'll never get well"; "I'll never get over this (whatever the disappointment is)"; "I'll never get love"; "I'll never find friends," and so on.) When you do that, you'll notice your mood drops immediately—way, way down to the floor.

Many people think (and say) this sentence many times a day: "I can't stand it!'—"it" being waiting on line, being snubbed, not being in charge, or any one of thousands of little annoyances we all endure. But "I can't stand it" is a strong phrase; when said aloud, you can almost feel your toes curl. It's so *final*. It precludes flexibility or acceptance. Those who use this phrase often are (or they soon become) tense, rigid people.

If this sentence keeps cropping up in your vocabulary, you might want to consider changing it to something less formidable, something that expresses your sentiment yet leaves room for change. "I don't like it, but that's the way it is." Or toy with a different concept: "Sure, I don't like it, but what the hell. I can take it; I've got more guts than they think . . ." and so on.

The words you choose when you talk to yourself are very, very important. And it's not just a question of idle semantics: Because words are the tools we humans use to help shape our thoughts.

I recently had occasion to talk to one of our former clients, a woman who had taken this program at its very beginning. She hadn't been homebound, but she was very limited in her travel. She belonged to the PTA—and when she'd go to meetings, she would sit way back in the last row, right near the door. (We all know why . . . don't we??) Well, it was a long climb up, but she's in excellent health, enjoys a good social life—*and* she's now president of the PTA!

We spoke about her new life and responsibilities and she told me how much pleasure she derives from having achieved something far beyond her wildest dreams. She told me how, often, when she's on stage, she looks toward the back of the auditorium and marvels at how far she's come. I asked her if she ever gets panic attacks now. She said, "No—but every time I drive by a certain street, I still get a little of that old anxiety feeling." I asked her why, and she said, "Well, that's where it all started, where I first got the panic attack that made me go through four long, miserable years." Both places—the auditorium and that particular street—were strongly associated in her mind with suffering. Yet (as I pointed out to her) look at the difference in her thinking! In one place she's saying things like: "Wow, who would ever have believed I'd be standing up here on the platform . . . ?" And: "I've come a long way, baby . . ." But in the other place, she still sees that street as the start of her "four long, miserable years."

It is any wonder some of that old feeling creeps back?

One woman called me on the phone recently to find out about the PASS-Group program. She told me she had had a "massive panic attack" about a week before, and that she had been in a terrible state ever since. She had been scheduled to have a laparotomy done because of abdominal pain. (This is a procedure where the doctor looks into the abdomen through a small incision.) This woman had already made arrangements to have someone look after her two children, but on the day she was supposed to enter the hospital, she had the panic attack. In telling me her story, she kept referring to this procedure as "going under." This was the phrase she used over and over again ("I had my children all prepared, but when the day came, I couldn't go under," and "they wanted me to go under"). I pointed out to her the loaded words she was using; she wasn't even aware she was doing it! "Anybody," I said, "would be afraid if they thought they were going under." But what special significance did the phrase have for her, I asked. "Being raped or drowning," was her answer.

The hospital said they'd reschedule her for another day. I spoke to her at length and told her that the next time she should think of the event as merely a diagnostic procedure—which is exactly what it is. She was greatly relieved. "I'm so glad I spoke to you," she told me again and again, "I feel a lot better already."

Do you see the enormous power that words have?

A Magic Phrase

I once read a story about a paratrooper in World War II. Each time, as he'd jump out of the plane and pull the ripcord, he'd say to himself, in a sort of magical incantation, "Well, here goes nothing." What he meant was: "Well, so what? This can't be helped. I'm here, I have to do this, I lived my life, it was a good life." So, those few words, "Well, here goes nothing," would give him courage.

Regina (whose story is included in the book), adopted as her motto, "I can do it." Here's a woman, by the way, who's in her mid-sixties. She suffered from panic attacks for the past twenty years. She could barely leave her home to do the marketing. Many times, she told me, she'd have to sit in the car, unable to leave it, while her husband would be in the store, shopping. This summer, about a year after she told her story for the book, she and her husband went on an extended vacation trip. They live in New Hampshire and they drove all the way to Utah to visit their granddaughter. From there, they went to California, then took the southern route back and stopped in Arizona to visit the Grand Canyon. They also went to Washington, D.C., to attend a wedding. Regina enjoyed her trip all the way—she had a ball! How was she able to do it? By following the program and saying to herself (and believing it): "I can do it. I'm well."

Here are a few other examples of what we might call (forgive the pun), "PASS words": One man, who studies metaphysics now, adopted one of the affirmations he heard about. Before he leaves his house, he says, "I go now to meet my good." One woman is comforted by reciting the Lord's Prayer. Another tells me she says to herself, "I'm surrounded by a healing light." One woman even told me her panic attacks began to go away for good after she told herself, "Hey, this is all a bunch of garbage."

So, you see, anything goes . . .

Try to find a magic phrase of your own that you can say to yourself in moments of stress—that will comfort you, yet, at the same time, give you the courage you need.

There's nothing wrong with this kind of help. In fact, there's everything right about it—from a psychological as well as a physiological standpoint—because you're not relying on drugs; you're relying on yourself. You're relying on your own inner thoughts to bring you peace and comfort. You're drawing on sources of courage and strength that are available to anyone who can read and think and learn.

CHAPTER 9

Step 5: Imagination

"Imagination is more important than
knowledge."

—*Albert Einstein*

IMAGINATION IS one of the most powerful of human attributes. Without it, civilization itself would have been impossible. But, like any other powerful tool, it can be used to create—or destroy.

You have an excellent imagination. We know that. (Aren't you always creating, in your mind, vivid disaster scenes?) But why not use this great gift of imagination to help yourself instead of hindering yourself?

The Act-As-If Principle

Earlier, we talked about how the things we believe in can affect us; how the sentry in the brain can become aroused or calmed by a belief.

But this is the most amazing part: Even if we only pretend to believe in something it can still exert an effect on us.

When Dr. Keith W. Sehnert, author of *How To Be Your Own Doctor—Sometimes*, was interviewed on the *Tonight Show*, he said afterward: "I had a real feeling of panic as I stood behind the curtain and listened to Ed McMahon introduce me as the next guest of Johnny Carson. I thought to myself, 'What in the world am I doing here with about fifteen million people watching!' Then, in a split second, the solution came. I said, 'You have two options: You can either blow it by looking at Carson as a big celebrity—or you can pretend you're just talking to a man from Nebraska who grew up with a lot of the same people you know.' I took the latter path, and we got along fine. People who saw me that night said, 'You didn't look a bit scared!' And I wasn't!"*

I (SSJ) had switched careers and started my medical training rather late in life. When I graduated from medical school, I was about fifty. Someone asked me, "How were you able to do this at your age?" And I replied, "It was easy. I just pretended I was thirty."

In French, there's a saying: "The appetite comes with the eating." You start with a simple action, pretending, if you have to. And as you continue with the action, things just follow along in the same path. The action picks up momentum. It becomes stronger and stronger.

Do you want to be more courageous? Then *act* as if you have courage.

What Would So-and-So Do?

Suppose you don't feel confident. It doesn't matter. Just act the part anyway. Is there someone you know whom you'd like to emulate, to copy? Perhaps a famous person, a teacher—or even the Person-You-Would-Like-to-Become. Just pretend you're that person already.

What purpose does it serve? It can get you over some pretty rough spots. It can also give you a welcome respite from always thinking of yourself and your problems. It can give you a new frame of reference, a new perspective. And the more you act like a confident person, the sooner you'll become one.

One of my clients once told me she was in a situation where she formerly experienced great panic. But instead of reacting, she asked herself instead, "Now, what would Shirley have done in this case?" She did it and she was just fine. What I really might have done in the same situation is unimportant. What is important is that this

*Reprinted by permission, *stress/unstress*, by Keith W. Sehnert, M.D., copyright © 1981, Augsburg Publishing House, Minneapolis.

woman projected, in her own mind, an idealized version of someone else—and she pretended that she was that person. And she acted accordingly.

I've used this strategy many times myself. I'd ask, "Now, what would a confident person do?" And I'd create a fictitious, confident person in my mind. I'd picture myself as that person. But, as I pointed out to my client, don't forget to give yourself credit for acting well in those circumstances. After all—it was still *you* who did it!

Once in a while, someone will ask a question like this: "Well, if I act confident when I'm really not, wouldn't that mean I'm denying my feelings? Wouldn't that be lying to myself?"

No, you're not denying your own feelings by acting bravely. You're not pushing down the fear, repressing it, or refusing to face it. On the contrary, you are facing the fact that you have this fear. You freely admit it. But then, you go on to make a conscious decision: Given this fear, what'll I do about it? If I act afraid, my fear will probably intensify. But if I act as if I'm brave, it'll help me and I'll be proud of myself. So therefore, I choose to act with courage. I'll act as if I'm brave. Notice the element of choice here. The person faces the facts (i.e., he confronts his own feelings), and on that basis, he makes a choice.

Applied Fantasy

Fantasy can be a most helpful tool. It allows you to explore new pathways and responses. I use the word *pathways* advisedly. Thinking involves linking neurons with other neurons. And when you do that, you create new patterns—hence new ways of looking at the same thing.

Sir Francis Galton, a British scientist (who, incidentally was a cousin of Charles Darwin), wrote in 1883 about the important influence of thought and memory in everyday behavior. Real or imaginary sights and sounds, he wrote, can impress themselves on the human mind and mold its reaction. The images can surround a physiological function with an aura of pain or pleasure so vivid, he said, that it can be associated with changed reflexes. Later, of course, Pavlov confirmed this in his famous experiment with the salivating dogs and the bells.

Yes, we all have a rich fantasy life. It's just a matter of putting it to good use. Here are some examples:

Sometimes when there are many problems in my life all at once and I (SAS) can't fall asleep easily, I pretend I'm a little baby lying in my crib with my mommy and daddy looking at me, admiring me, cooing at me, loving me. Pretty soon, my problems melt away . . . I'm a baby again and I go peacefully to sleep.

One of our counselors advises her clients to think of themselves as a car. A car, she explains, will not run unless it gets proper fuel—and you can't run it indefinitely without some rest. If something goes wrong, a red light goes on to warn you. That means you have to correct those conditions if you want to get good mileage out of your car.

One woman was asked to accompany her child's class on a picnic that involved a boat ride. She was terrified of the boat ride because she wouldn't be in control. (How would she get to shore if she panicked?) In addition to the first aid treatment (just in case), she decided to use the following fantasy: She would become the owner of that boat! Because in her boat, she was in control. I asked her, "But why stop with one boat? Why not get yourself a whole fleet of boats?" "Sure," she laughed, "why not??" P.S. The trip went very well, No problem. She had a wonderful time and her daughter was happy Mom could come.

Another woman had to go to a party given by her husband's boss. It was to be a very formal affair with many important people present—and she was scared. I happened to mention the story of the woman and her boats—and she decided to use the same strategy: She would own the ballroom! She reported, the following week, that she had a really marvelous time at the party. She walked in, she said, like a queen.

The Olympic Gold Medal champion skier Jean-Claude Killy learned to ski as a small boy. He never had a formal lesson, but he would watch the Olympic skiers in his native village—and he'd imitate them. As he'd ski down the slopes, he pretended he was one of them. And, of course, the day came when he was!

Here's what one client told us: "I was in this store, and I began to feel jittery. Anyhow, I was reaching for my wallet to pay for the things I bought, when I suddenly got this idea. My counselor had always told me to use my imagination in a good way, and also to bring something along from home when I go out. Anyhow, I saw my girlfriend's picture in my wallet—she's this girl I like from school—and I imagined myself being with her. I pictured her scared, and me saying, 'It's okay, I'm here for you. I won't let anything hurt you.' And that's what made me feel better right away. When I thought of somebody else being scared, that helped me forget my own fears. So I've continued to use this same strategy, even when I'd go out driving in the car. I'd stop every now and then, open my wallet, look at her picture, and continue on my way. I don't have to turn back again and run home, the way I used to."

Dr. Toni Grant, the well-known psychologist, once offered this fear-reducing technique: Instead of struggling to push the fear out of your mind (which we know doesn't work), simply let go of that effort to keep the fear in. But use imagery. Locate the feeling in a certain part of your body. (Where is it—your tummy? Your middle? Your chest?) Then, she said, make that fear bigger; feel that area of your body expand and grow. Know it's only a feeling—and you're controlling it by changing its size. When the area gets large enough, visualize doors and windows in that area of your body. Open wide these imaginary doors and windows—and let the fear escape through these openings. Try it and see if it works for you.

One client told me he visualizes the sentry in his brain

as another person who lives inside him. Sometimes, he said, he pictures this person, this sentry, sitting next to him in a chair. In his mind, he talks to him. He asks him what he wants; how they can cooperate together or how he might reassure this sentry.

Sometimes someone will ask: If I talk to myself and fantasize and pretend, couldn't I become crazy? No. As we pointed out before, psychosis is a whole different ballgame. First of all, in these little head games, you're not substituting fantasy for reality. You're helping yourself cope with reality by redefining it temporarily, to be more in line with the actions you want to assume. And, secondly, you're fantasizing at will.

Come to think of it, aren't billion-dollar industries—the entertainment industry, for example—built around this very concept? Haven't you ever cried, watching a movie or reading a book? You knew the stories weren't real, yet you reacted to some degree as if they were. Of course, the emotional impact isn't as strong as when it happens to us in real life. Nonetheless, something important is going on: Some physical changes were taking place, brain chemicals were being manufactured. Imagination is a powerful force in our lives, for good or ill. We all spend a good part of our day imagining and pretending all sorts of things. We do this because we have a large brain that begs constant input.

Those what-if thoughts you're entertaining all the time (and maybe they're not so entertaining!) are destructive—not because they're fantasy, but because they interfere with your functioning in the real world. Fantasy put to good use, on the other hand, enhances your performance in the real world.

"Dr. Cricket"

Many of our clients have told us that they'd been programmed for years to "hear" a negative "voice" inside their heads: "Don't do this . . . stay away from that . . . what will people think . . . what if this, what if that . . ."

One of the best "therapists" around is a fellow named Jiminy Cricket. (Do you remember him from the Walt Disney movie *Pinocchio*?) He's a whimsical little character, about five inches tall; he wears a suit and tie and a high hat, and carries a green umbrella. He can easily perch on your shoulder, and you just carry him around with you, wherever you go. You can project all these negative "voices" on to him—like a ventriloquist. Somehow, when Jiminy Cricket makes these dire pronouncements, they don't sound nearly as threatening as when, for example, it's your mother who "says" them!

"I laughed so hard," a client told us, "when I thought of Jiminy Cricket sitting on my shoulder. You know, I always heard my mother's voice inside my head telling me, don't say this because if you do, they can turn right around and say that to you. Things like that. So that always used to inhibit me. I couldn't speak out. I was always afraid of saying the wrong thing. But now with this little creature on my shoulder, even if he tells me not to say things, he's so comical, I can't take him seriously, and I start to laugh. I find myself speaking up much more these days."

Heat Application

Heat expands not only metal, but muscles, too. When muscles are cold, they contract.* Expanded muscles are associated with warmth and relaxation. (Think of a cat sitting square in the wintertime and all stretched out, as if poured out on the floor, in the summertime.)

So one of the ways to relax and stretch out your muscles is to Think Heat. Even if the heat and warmth aren't really there, you can bring them in your imagination!

See yourself lying comfortably on the beach. Think of the sun, shining warmly on your arms or neck or back—anywhere you feel muscle tension.

---

*That's what shivering is all about; the muscles are being contracted. But contracting muscles are working muscles, and when they work, they produce heat. So it all evens out.

Or think back to your childhood. When you were sick and needed something warm, what did your mother bring you? Was it a water bottle? A blanket? A warm compress? A heating pad? Think back. Whatever it was that brought you warmth and comfort then—try to see it now. Imagine it vividly in front of you. Now, place this heat object directly on the group of muscles that feels tight or tense. Hold it there for several minutes or as long as you want to.

An Experiment

If you'd like further proof of what a powerful tool imagination can be, are you game for an experiment?

Have someone read the following script to you. (Or make a tape recording yourself.) Speak in a calm, clear, natural manner. As you listen to the words, imagine that whatever is being said is actually happening:

SCRIPT*: "I am going to close my eyes now. I close them and let myself really feel how tightly shut my eyes can feel. As I let myself experience my eyes tightly closed, they begin to feel more and more tightly shut . . . as if they were stuck tight . . . very heavy, very tightly closed. . . . I am going to let my eyes close more and more tightly now with every breath I breathe out. . . . I can feel them closing tighter and tighter shut. . . .

"I can use my imagination to really build up this stuck-tight feeling . . . so I am imagining that someone is taking a special magic surgical glue and puts one drop on my upper eyelid and one drop on my lower eyelid, and I tell myself I can feel this glue taking effect now . . . becoming very, very sticky . . . gluing my eyes tightly shut . . . as if they were one piece of skin . . . covering my eyes . . . glued closed now . . . I let myself really feel it now, more and more. . . .

"To make doubly certain that my eyes feel stuck tightly

*From the book, *Strategic Self-Hypnosis*, by Robert A. Strauss, Ph.D. © 1982. Reprinted by permission of the publisher, Prentice-Hall, Inc., Englewood Cliffs, NJ 07632.

shut, they are taking some chewing gum and working a gooey wad over my right eye and my left eye . . . really working it into my eyelashes . . . so they become all gooed up . . . very sticky . . . sealing my eyes shut . . . all gummed up . . . I can feel that my eyelid muscles feel too weak to tug my eyes open . . . they can't open against this sticky gum . . . sealed tightly shut now . . . I can really feel it. . . .

"And they are now taking some package-sealing tape, just to make sure, and a six-inch-long strip of superstrong package-sealing tape is being stuck over my right eye now . . . and now my left eye . . . and I can feel them taping my eyes shut and I can really feel it . . . shut . . . sealed . . . glued and taped shut. . . . I can feel my eyes stuck more and more tightly closed . . . stuck tighter and tighter with every breath I breathe in, more and more impossible to force open with every breath I breathe out . . . it feels more and more like it would be useless to try pulling my eyes open now. . . .

"My eyes are stuck so very tightly shut now. . . . I can really feel it . . . feel them glued and gummed and taped shut . . . and the more I try to force my eyelids to open, the more they fight to stay shut. . . . I can feel it more and more now . . . more and more. . . . I keep thinking about and feeling this stuck-tight feeling. . . .

"While I keep telling myself my eyes are stuck tightly closed . . . and I keep my mind thinking and feeling and picturing and imagining how they are glued and gummed and taped so they couldn't possibly open, I will try as hard as I can to force them to open anyhow. . . .

"It's useless, but I will try now to force my eyelids apart . . . they feel odder and odder, the harder I try. . . . I can feel it in my eyebrows and my forehead . . . my eyes feel glued and gummed and taped all the way shut . . . so tightly they feel numb . . . they just don't seem to want to open . . . but I try to make them open anyway. . . . I can't . . . they're stuck tight. . . .

"I try harder. . . . I strain to force them open . . . to pull my eyelids apart . . . the harder I try the more tightly they stick, they just don't seem to want to open. . . .

"But now I'm going to stop trying to open my eyes. . . . I

just relax and let my eyes and my eyelids relax . . . the
stuck feelings all go away . . . the tape and the glue and
the gum feelings all go away now. . . . I know I can open
my eyes if I just allow them to open . . . all by themselves. . . . I just allow my eyes to pop open naturally
and automatically . . . the experiment is over and I can
once again allow my eyes to open."

If you've chosen to do this experiment, what did you
feel toward the end? If you've done it correctly, you had
great difficulty in opening up your eyes.

That's because you've created a double-bind, no-win
situation! You tried to force your eyes open while telling
yourself and believing they were tightly closed. The situation you created in your mind was one in which it was
impossible to open your eyes. (How could you open
them if they were glued shut with such a strong glue?)
Straining and forcing while that image was vividly before
you only brought more tension. But the minute you
relaxed and let go of that image, you were able to open
your eyes with ease.

Somewhere along the line, as a result of imprinting by
shock, you've made an "I-swear" decision *not* to go
beyond a certain area, beyond a certain well-defined
perimeter. You've hypnotized yourself (through self-
suggestion reinforced countless times) into believing that
if you go there, something disastrous might happen. And
you've kept that promise because it was a decision you
yourself made.

Isn't it time now to dehypnotize yourself? Those prom-
ises you made to yourself—I won't go beyond this
point—up to here, and no further—are really not in your
best interests.

That I-can't-go-beyond-X is only glue on your eyelids.
As long as the glue remains, it's hard to get unstuck.

CHAPTER 10

Step 6: Social Support

"Loneliness is something that causes us
to take the risks and to move out.
So there's a very *positive* aspect to loneliness; don't be afraid to feel it."
—*Dr. Leo Buscaglia*

THERE'S NO getting away from it: We humans belong to a
social species—which means that in order to remain
normal and healthy, we need the company of others.
Naturally, there are individual differences. Some of us,
by nature, are more outgoing and require more social
contact. But we all need some sense of social connectedness, of being valued as a friend, of being socially viable
in a positive way.

One of the reasons for the general malaise in our
modern cities and suburbs is the lack of opportunity for
many satisfying social contacts on a daily basis. When
you take large groups of people and you put each one (or
each couple) in an isolated unit; when you stack these
units vertically (in apartments) or horizontally (in private
homes) without any interconnectedness of any kind, surely
the inhabitants of these boxlike structures will experience
a sense of deprivation, especially since, according to one
survey, the average American moves fourteen times in a
lifetime.

Fear of Rejection

The fear of rejection seems to be an inborn human
characteristic—almost like an involuntary knee-jerk reflex. This has to do with the long history of socialization

that our species has gone through. If everybody just did his own thing, without regard to how his behavior affected others, how would mankind ever have formed cohesive tribes and groups?

To an extent the fear of rejection occurs in other species that have been domesticated. A dog, for instance, will tolerate physical pain with great forbearance if he knows his master is on his side. But a dog will cringe in fear (and obvious emotional anguish) if you censure him with cross words or even a look.

The late Dr. Hans Selye writes in *The Stress of Life*:

> . . . . As much as we thirst for approval, we dread censure. The common statement, "I don't care what anybody says" is almost invariably untrue. Probably I should not have said "almost," because I do not know of a single person who does not care what anybody says. Is this pretense necessary? If a person is quite certain he is right (which is rarely the case among intelligent people), he should stick to his guns no matter how much he is criticized. Many strong people can do this. But no one is indifferent to censure. Why pretend not to care about criticism? Those who are honest with themselves know very well that they would rather be approved than criticized.

So, while a watered-down version of the fear of rejection may be an asset to human development, if carried to an extreme, it becomes a definite liability.

Dr. Rochelle Myers once remarked, "If you don't get rejected at least three times a day, you're not living creatively." She humorously emphasized a very important point: That being rejected is *not* synonymous with failing. Quite the contrary. In order to live creatively (and who doesn't want to do that?), we must take risks. And when we take risks—when we try new things, when we stick our neck out, when we reach out to others—we *may* be rejected. After all, there are so many people and so many ways of thinking, and so many opinions—that whatever we do, we're bound to step on somebody's toes sometimes. We can't please everyone. So, what we have to do is make allowances for these rejections—and realize that they're only a concomitant of risk-taking. Everyone has to contend with that in one form or another. Why take it so personally? Why get so upset about it?

As I've (SSJ) mentioned, I started my medical training rather late in life. After I graduated medical school, I found it difficult to get a residency because of my age. I figured maybe one out of a hundred hospitals would take me on. So when the letters started coming back saying they wouldn't accept me, I merely kept count. I wasn't unduly concerned about all the negative answers. (Let's face it: I wasn't jumping for joy, either. But I was not unduly concerned.) In fact, the more letters I received, the closer I felt I was to my goal—that letter from the hundredth hospital that would accept me, despite my age. My patience paid off; I eventually did get not one but several letters of acceptance.

The reason I had this positive attitude was because I didn't consider the letters I received as rejection letters. In other words, they weren't really rejecting me, as a person. The negative responses merely reflected the reality of the situation, because, statistically speaking, it *is* harder to secure a position like this at a later age. But harder doesn't mean impossible. And it was nothing personal. So I saw no reason to feel that I failed or that it was my fault. It was this realistic evaluation that helped me stay calm and maintain a positive attitude.

Salespeople have to take something of this stance, too. They have to realize that not everybody is going to buy their products. And they have to set sales goals for themselves that reflect the nature of their product. For example, if you're selling hot dogs in a ballpark, you're going to have many customers in one hour; if you're selling apartment buildings, you may only have one customer a year! Acquiring friends is a little like that, too. If you have one or two real friends in a lifetime, they say, you're ahead of the game!

Many sensitive people, in an effort to spare themselves the emotional suffering of criticism or rejection, withdraw from life. But while this may seem to be the less painful solution, in the end they only suffer more—again, because we are basically social creatures. So the benefits are only temporary and short-lived.

Obviously, one way to overcome this is to become more friendly yourself. (You're telling people, in effect, "See? I won't bite!")

The fear of rejection has still another face to it: A person who feels vulnerable and insecure very often dislikes and rejects others who display or remind him of similar traits. (That's why children are often so cruel to their peers. They themselves feel so small and vulnerable.) But the interesting thing is that when a person increases his self-esteem through growth and self-knowledge, he very often, as a result, becomes much more tolerant—not only of himself, but of others, too.

Even if you're born with a thin skin and are easily hurt and bruised, you have to develop a tougher outside shell, so refusals and rejections don't hurt as much. You can refuse, too—refuse to be hurt or intimidated by a no answer. Simply chalk it up to the law of percentages—and go on from there.

Creating a Bond

There is a constant interaction between any living organism and its environment. The organism will push itself against its environment, so to speak, and the environment will push itself against it. When the environment is too threatening, too overpowering, the organism retreats as a survival measure. On the other hand, if the environment is favorable, if it is approving and permissive, then the organism expands toward the outer limits of its inborn capacity. This applies to all life, from the simplest creatures to man.

Therefore, if you perceive your environment (that is, the people in it) to be hostile and menacing, then it's up to you to find a way out. You cannot expect your soul to expand in a cold, hostile place. Even a plant needs warmth and nourishment. You also need the warmth of a touch, a good word, a stroke now and then. You must form a bonding with someone, somewhere. You have to provide an environment in which your soul can expand.

Don't think this is impossible. There are hundreds of millions of people and animals sharing this planet. Surely, among all those living beings you can find those few with whom you can establish a rapport.

Retreating, withdrawing from life, running away from social contacts and commitments, may seem to be the less painful solution. But in the end, the price you pay for such behavior is enormous. Realize this: The benefits you derive by retreating and withdrawing are only temporary and short-lived. They are not the long-term answer.

Deflecting Attention Outwardly

So many people who suffer from agoraphobia tend to look inward too much, to dwell on minor physical variations of the norm, to notice each breath, each heartbeat. In short: they give in too much to the hypochondriacal tendencies most of us have. Yet, how much more profitable it would be to deflect some of this attention outwardly, to other people, animals, hobbies. To the world of ideas and books. To nature. Science. To literature, art, music, sports. To something outside the self.

One of our clients had a sudden insight one day while riding the subway. "The panic attacks are more apt to come," she wrote, "when you think too much about what goes on inside—and not enough about what goes on outside."

When you deflect your attention outwardly, you not only help get rid of the panic attacks, but you stand to gain an important fringe benefit as well: You become a far more interesting person to be with! And when you meet people in social situations and you start focusing on how to put *them* at ease, it may give you still another fringe benefit. It may make you very popular.

Strokes

Some years ago, Dr. Eric Berne, founder of Transactional Analysis, refined the vague term, "social interaction," and honed it down to something specific. He called it "strokes." All higher primates, he pointed out, groom and stroke each other's fur as a means of social communication. We're primates, too—and we have the same need for stroking. But we can do it with words. "Anything that says to another, 'I know you're there, I recognize you,' is a stroke," he said. "These needs are part of our biological and psychological hungers—and these hungers can be satisfied with strokes."

Here's a common, everyday example of what Dr. Berne means. Say you step outside and you see your next-door neighbor. You stop and chat for a while, about the weather—or anything. It really doesn't matter. The important thing is that you've made social contact. So you walk away with that little glow, that sense of being socially connected. It may seem to be trivial. But it's not. It's very important.

Here's what Donald B. Ardell, author of *High Level Wellness* writes with a little bit of tongue-in-cheek:

> Based upon incredibly complicated, extraordinarily scientific, and wonderfully intuitive reasoning, I have personally determined that you need not less than 6.5 hugs and/or warm strokes daily. More than this number will do you no harm; in fact, I recommend you get, and give, as many as you can while getting on with the affairs of the day.

When you get—and give—strokes, you help dispel your anxiety, your tension, your fear. This helps you lower even further your chances of having a panic attack.

Here I must interject a little story that illustrates how far away we've come in our society from the good, ordinary, simple human contacts that many other people around the globe take for granted; and that we, in our rich society, have to painfully relearn.

One of our clients, a young man of nineteen, had been practically housebound when he joined this program. His sister lived about a mile away, in Brooklyn, and when he was able to leave his house more freely, he decided, as one of his assignments, to visit his sister. He was somewhat concerned that he might feel lightheaded or strange while walking, so, in addition to the usual advice about food and relaxation, I also told him to stop to say something to somebody if he feels this way—to ask directions, or the time—just to establish that human contact.

He later told me what happened. He was passing a housing project surrounded by a large open area. He began to feel a little giddy, so he looked around and the only person he saw was an elderly man sitting on a bench near one of the buildings. So my client walked up to him. But when the old man saw this tall, husky teenager in sneakers approaching him, *he* panicked!

Being Able to Trust

Psychologists often speak of the ability to establish trust as one of the hallmarks of the mature person. This may be true—but the question is: Whom will you trust? There are many people out there in the world; there are a lot of good people and there are a lot of bad people. No reasonably intelligent person today would just trust everybody, indiscriminately. To think otherwise is quite naive. But since we're social beings, we certainly have to trust some people and establish bonds with them.

Some of you may have been so hurt by someone that you learned your lesson and decided never to trust anyone. But this, too, is an irrational viewpoint. Not wanting to trust anyone is a very painful way to resolve a once-received hurt. If you continue with this viewpoint, you'll only end up the loser—because you'll have missed out on many wonderful friendships along the way. Friends help us achieve a greater degree of security, peace of mind and contentment.

Even temporary bondings are important, as I told my nineteen-year-old client. I remember, many years ago, having a panic attack in the subway. I was holding on to the strap, wondering if I'd ever get out of there alive. A woman who was sitting near me leaned over to me, smiled and said, "It's all right, dear. Don't worry." Something inside of me immediately relaxed.

Wanting to Belong

Wanting to belong is a very powerful human urge. Yet many people, unfortunately, don't see it this way at all. They see their loneliness as something to be ashamed of, to hide from the world. They don't see this longing for human contact as a normal, human feeling, but as a shortcoming that they themselves must somehow overcome. So they turn even more inward and try to develop their own resources as a substitute for friends.

This, we feel, is a great mistake. Not that you shouldn't develop your own resources—of course you should! But, paradoxically, these can best—or possibly, only—be developed within the framework and context of social interchange and social connections!

I know of an only child (now a happily married young woman) who, in her loneliness in childhood, reached out to correspond with pen pals from all over the world. She still maintains, to this day, her friendships with the girls she used to write letters to, in England, Japan, India, and Australia. She's built up friendships and travel enjoyment for years to come.

Love-Rays

Did you know that falling in love makes the body produce more endorphins (the good body chemicals)? That's why we feel so high, so terrific, when we're in love. The whole word is suddenly brighter: The grass is greener, the sky, bluer. Even rainy days are shiny. And the little things that used to annoy you don't bother you anymore.

Love, you know, isn't only sexual. It's friendly feelings

intensified, a kind of giving. You can not only love your mate, but you can love your friends, your children, your dog, your cat.

I remember my dog, Jenee, a gray poodle. Often, as I'd be sitting in my chair, reading, I'd look up from time to time and catch her staring at me. Such love would emanate from her eyes, it made me think of rays, zapping me with love.

See What Happens

You, too, can give the people in your life rays. Turn them on one day and see what happens.

Maybe in the outside world you've learned to be:

>Cautious instead of Friendly;
>Reserved instead of Enthusiastic;
>Shy instead of Outgoing.

If that's how you've been behaving, you probably haven't been receiving your share of the recognition and satisfaction you deserve.

See for yourself how it feels to be friendly, enthusiastic, and outgoing. Just try it on for size. If it fits, fine. If not—what have you got to lose? You can always go back to the way you were before.

So—during this time period—ACT AS IF you're already a friendly, enthusiastic, and outgoing person. ACT AS IF you really want to help and be nice to all the people you meet. Please do it even if you think you can't or even if you feel it's insincere, since you may not know the other person. Don't let that stop you. Do it anyway. Don't wait for someone else to do it—you do it first.

Starting a Social Network in Your Own Neighborhood

It's really not that difficult to start a social network— once you put your creative talents to work! Almost all communities, however small, have a newspaper—and you can place a little ad there. (Not to advertise overtly for friends; that would be so obvious that it wouldn't work!) Start a special interest group around your hobbies and interests. For example: sewing club; arts and crafts; baby-care club (where you read and discuss appropriate books); general discussion club; gardening club; weekly religious readings; rap group; and so on.

Your ad can simply read: Discussion Club—and you give your telephone number. (If you're reluctant about inviting strangers into your home, you can screen the calls when they answer the ad.) All you'd need to start a club are just two other people. I (SAS) started a very successful neighborhood Discussion Club, using this same method. Two people answered my ad—and from this small beginning, the Club grew to a dozen members. And now, after several years, it's still going strong!

I knew a woman who started a sewing club in the apartment building where she lives. One day, she tacked a notice about the club near the mailbox. Two tenants responded. One tenant had a friend in a nearby building who was interested; the other knew of a relative. So little by little, the group grew in size.

About a year later, I went to a local art show and was delighted to meet this woman again at one of the booths. By then, the group had become professional. They were all making beautiful projects, such as needlework and dolls. The entire group's work was on display, and many of the things were for sale. This woman— the founder of the club, who once suffered from phobias—told me she felt great. And why not? She had new friends, new interests, and a much healthier attitude!

Your meetings can be held in members' homes on a rotating basis. You can plan to have weekly, bi-monthly, or even monthly meetings. This outlet can afford you great pleasure and be a source of an increasing network of friends.

From there, you can branch out to other areas. Once you become more mobile, many other opportunities will surely present themselves: other clubs to join, classes to attend, and more. Your interests will by then be directed more outwardly, so you'll be hearing a lot more about these community activities.

The main thing is to recognize how important it is to have a social network.

A Courage Workshop

If you'd like to form a phobia support group, we can offer you some general guidelines. Incidentally, to avoid the negative-sounding name, "phobia group," why not call it a Courage Workshop instead?

Attracting membership is going to have to be the first step. To round out your membership, you might want to include members who have simple phobias, those whose fears center around one particular area and are not necessarily related to random panic attacks. The seven steps outlined in this book would be very helpful to them, as well.

To get the group started, a first step would be to place a notice in your local newspaper. Perhaps run the ad more than once. Or you can make a few flyers to post in supermarkets, libraries, or community bulletin boards. (If you're homebound, you can mail them to these places.) The flyers or ads can be very simple; they needn't say very much. Perhaps something like this:

> Are panic attacks or phobias
> interfering with your life?
>
> Join Our COURAGE WORKSHOP
> For information, call:
> XXXXXXXX

Screen the calls carefully, especially if you plan to have meetings at members' homes. Don't be afraid to talk to your callers at length and ask questions.

Before PASS came into existence, I organized a neighborhood antistress club. The purpose was to get together with other women, not only as a social club, but also to help each other with problems as they arise. As it turned out, most of the problems centered around fear: for example, fear of public speaking, fear of being alone, fear of making a fool of oneself. This group, as you'll soon see, was the forerunner of PASS.

One day, we were all sitting around my big kitchen table. One of the women brought up the matter of her problem: She couldn't ride on buses. Someone asked her why, and she said every time she'd get on a bus, she'd get a panic attack. That was why she stopped going on buses. I asked the women in the group—there were ten of us at the time—if anybody has ever had a panic attack. Slowly, every hand in the room went up.

We looked at each other—and burst out laughing. Here we were—a group of normal, average neighborhood women—yet each of us had experienced episodes of unprovoked panic! Unless there was something wrong with the Law of Averages, I thought, this problem is very, very common. Yet, each of us though we were the only ones. And we were ashamed to admit it: "What would people think?"

And what became of the woman who was afraid to go on the bus? She was instantly cured! The bus episodes had happened to her some years before—and all this time she avoided buses. Our meeting happened to be on a Tuesday; every Wednesday she went to play bingo. But the following day, her husband was unable to drive her there. She decided to go there anyhow—by bus. She figured: If panic is so common and everybody has it, why should I worry? So she went and had a very enjoyable evening. Ever since then, she has never minded having to take the bus.

But there's even an addendum to the story: She also got over her fear of flying! Several months later, she went down to Florida—for the first time—to visit her mother!

We had many other success stories. One of our members, Rose, had a great fear of driving—although she did have a driver's license. She was a widow, and for the four years since her husband died, she had been totally dependent on her sister to drive her to the supermarket, the doctor's office—everywhere. And, meanwhile, her car was right there, in the garage; nobody was using it. The crisis came when her sister (who lived in the same building) planned to move to another state, where her daughter lived. Rose felt cornered; she was terror-stricken at the thought of having to drive. What we did at the club was this:

One of the members who lived several blocks away was to make a little party. The plan was to have Rose drive—by herself—to attend the party. A few people that Rose knew were invited to be the mystery guests. On the day of the party, just before leaving her house, Rose called me for reassurance, as we planned. Then she called the woman who was making the party. Rose knew there'd be a surprise there for her, but she didn't know what. That was part of the lure, the magnet, to get her to the party!

When she got there and rang the bell, there was that little welcoming group: "Surprise!" The house had been decorated. There was food and music. They all had a wonderful time. Rose drove by herself (as planned)—and that day marked the end of her fear of driving. This happened years ago, and Rose is now driving everywhere.

Another woman, Ellen, developed a fear of having guests come to her house. It seems that her husband, a very gregarious, outgoing fellow, used to invite people to come up for coffee all the time. Ellen was brought up in a household where they rarely had visitors. So she never learned the art of being a good hostess. She always felt inadequate when guests were there—simply because she didn't quite know what to do, how or what to serve.

So we helped her. We came to her house. With us, she had nothing to fear; it was already out in the open. We were the guests, and Ellen practiced serving us. We did this twice—and she successfully overcame her fears. Ellen mastered the new skill, and she no longer had to quarrel with her husband when he brought home unexpected guests.

Similarly, your club can also encompass other members, who may not suffer from spontaneous panic attacks—

but who have other fears that they want to do something about.

The Group: Some How-To Suggestions

If you're a small group, conducting the meetings on your own without professional help, you can just take turns being the leader. Or someone volunteers. You don't have to be formal about it; it's just to know that one person is there as a facilitator—to see that people speak without being interrupted, for example. If your group is a little larger and you would like to have more professional leadership, you might ask one of the teachers at your local school—or some other capable person—to volunteer to act as a facilitator. Since we provide you with information and a reading list, there would be no problem in terms of program material.

The only other word of advice is this: There are some people (fortunately, a small minority) who are filled with what I can only call negative energy. They simply drain you. They don't really want to get better—or help others to get better. Instead, they want to draw everybody down to their level—and make others feel as miserable as they feel.

I was once invited to sit in on a group therapy session for people who had phobias. It was supposedly led by a professional psychologist. I say supposedly because all he did was sit in a corner and take notes. One man (who loved to hear himself talk) dominated the conversation with complaints about his impossible mother-in-law. You can't have a successful group meeting when somebody dominates the conversation like this. And without an adequate group leader (if there are more than five people) to tie in the discussion, the meeting gets nowhere.

In order to be an effective, successful group, there has to be the generation of positive energy. When people see others getting better; when they realize there's hope; when they begin to view themselves as part of a group and not alone anymore—so many good things begin to happen in the group. On the other hand, if there's a lot of negative energy—if people just come to talk about symptoms and how miserable they feel or how they can't do this or that—if they come to meetings to gossip, or to put others down you can see that this group isn't going to be helpful to anybody.

What all this means is that certain rules have to be laid down at the beginning. For example, no discussion of symptoms. People who are prone to panic attacks are highly suggestible and more readily attuned to listen in and copy the symptoms they hear described.

Another rule would be to keep it confidential. You can't develop a trust in a group if people aren't sure their stories won't be carried all over town.

Each meeting would need a theme, a plan. This is very important, because otherwise the meeting flounders. That's why we're offering this guide to recovery, so your group members can follow it and make progress.

If you would like to form a larger group—or if your little group wants to grow—you might want to think about getting a church or other community organization to sponsor your group. Mary Ann Miller of Royal Oak, Michigan, a recovered agoraphobic, did just that. She is the founder of AIM (Agoraphobics in Motion). Her organization is based on Alcoholics Anonymous, and there are now several chapters in different cities.

There are pros and cons about having a smaller group that meets in members' homes versus a larger one that would meet, say, in a church basement. A smaller group, obviously, is more intimate. Friendships are more likely to form; there is a certain cohesiveness to the group that a larger group might lack. But that's if the people are truly compatible and like each other. If there is a lot of negative energy around, a larger group would be able to absorb it more easily. The negative energy would be diluted in the presence of many more people who would presumably be following the program.

But whether your organization is large or small, here are a few more ideas that we think might be helpful to you: (Some were suggested by Mary Ann Miller.)

Collecting Dues Instead of just passing around the hat, you'd be much better off charging each person $1 (or more) admission fee. This way, you'll soon have enough money in your treasury to do the things that will benefit the entire group:

1. You'll have more money for advertising (notices in local newspapers) to build up your club.
2. You can spend some of the money on parties and other social events of the club, like members' birthdays. Or you can have outings and picnics later on.

Welcoming New Members In a small group, there's usually no problem about introductions and newcomers; everyone knows what good manners call for. But as the group gets larger, it's very important that a welcoming procedure be established. Think of how you would feel if you walked into a room and didn't see one familiar face! Wouldn't it feel good if someone came over to you and introduced himself? So make sure this is being done in your group. Arrange to have a special welcoming committee; the task shouldn't fall only to one individual.

Membership Fee You would be better off, we feel, if you charged an initial lump sum for membership (in addition to the weekly dues). It might be only a nominal amount, and you could also have prospective members fill out an application form.

The purpose would be to weed out those people who are not serious about helping themselves and others—and those who might come merely to be entertained. (Yes, there are such people.) You might also have handy a special reference number of some community agency, to give to those people who may have serious mental problems—which you, of course, as a layman, cannot be expected to deal with.

A Reward System It's more fun and it works a lot better if each person has a specific goal in mind when he starts the program. This can be the basis for a gold star reward system. Psychologists have repeatedly demonstrated that learning takes place faster and better when there's a reward waiting at the end of the line, so to speak. But rewards are not only useful, they're fun!

One suggestion might be: Each member has a card with his goals written out on the card. As he reaches each goal, a star is pasted on the card. But the next step is even more important: Upon attaining his goal, he gets acknowledgement from the group.

Getting applause is an excellent way to acknowledge the efforts a person has made. Applause may seem to be a trivial thing, but it really isn't. We all thrive on demonstrated approval, strokes, rewards. They just make us feel good.

Mystery Phone Calls One of the things we found to be very enjoyable in our little antistress club a few years ago were the Mystery Phone Calls we started. They encouraged us to become more friendly with each other.

At each meeting, members wrote their names and phone numbers on slips of paper, folded them, and put them in a bowl. At the end of the meeting we would draw slips from the bowl. (If we picked our own name, we'd exchanged the slip with someone else.) We would have to call that person, whose name was on the slip, once during the week. Naturally, the name was kept secret, so it was a surprise.

Publicity Contact your local newspaper and see if they will do a little story about your group or about panic disorder. You might also get referrals for membership from a doctor or a hospital. In smaller communities, there might be free publicity on radio or even TV.

Frima Rosen, who does volunteer work for the Agoraphobic Foundation of Canada, and who has appeared on radio and TV on behalf of the organization, offers this advice for getting publicity:

Sometimes all you have to do is ask. You have to be "gutsy." You have to approach those people in the media and explain about agoraphobia and panic attacks. You have to let them know how many people it afflicts and how people are so debilitated by it. You have to impress upon them the need for awareness—not only for the public, but the medical profession, too. And they have to know there's help out there, other than medication.

Although Frima didn't actually start the group (it was Dr. Michael Spevack of Montreal General Hospital who did), she, her husband, and a small nucleus of volunteers are now working for the organization. This Canadian group has grown considerably; at meetings they can have anywhere from fifty, sixty, even one hundred people. And they get letters from all over Canada.

Guest speakers In addition to this book, you can also have speakers address your group from time to time. The speakers could be nutritionists from your local health department. Perhaps the high school football coach could give a talk on the importance of exercise. Maybe there's a qualified person in your community who can give a lecture on additional relaxation methods.

The possibilities are endless, once you create a good, positive let's-all-see-how-we-can-improve atmosphere.

If you prefer getting help on a one-to-one basis, by telephone, we invite you to contact PASS-Group.

CHAPTER 11

Step 7: Spiritual Values

"The answer is *not* religion . . . the
answer is a *relationship* with God."
—*Dr. Robet Schuller,*
minister and psychologist

EACH CULTURE, each civilization, takes the raw material
of human clay and shapes it to its needs. It's not that
human nature can be changed; it can't. It's just that each
society draws out and magnifies certain human traits,
while, at the same time, it subdues and inhibits others.

In the olden days, when bravery on the battlefield was
absolutely necessary for victory, courage was amply rewarded. And wherever it was rewarded and admired,
many became self-motivated to cultivate those traits in
themselves. If you've studied ancient Greece, you'll remember the city-state of Sparta. The Spartan way of life
was harsh to the extreme. Its people were tough as nails.
Self-discipline, bravery, and courage were overemphasized,
while the gentler, artistic aspects of life were sharply
suppressed. This is not to say, of course, that societal
extremes are to be admired; they're not. But we merely
want to point out how malleable human beings are and
how they can be molded by society.

History records that the Spartans were fearless fight-
ers. But this isn't entirely true. They were human beings,
like the rest of us. They, too, were afraid of danger,
death, fire, and so on. But they were taught, since early
childhood, to act with courage and stoicism in the face of
fear. And, in time, they developed traits of courage and
daring until these became second nature to them.

But what happens in our society today? In an age of
push-button warfare, governments don't particularly need

courageous citizens. In fact, courage is a hindrance to the politicians; they'd much prefer a docile, submissive population. Nowadays, when people do display acts of courage—as, for example, when someone sees a crime being committed and rushes in to save the victim—is such a noble act rewarded? Not only isn't it rewarded, but the hero is even punished for his heroism! (He has to appear in court to testify; lose time for work; face possible revenge by the released and angered criminal; and so forth.) Thus, unintentionally, perhaps, the noble trait of courage is quietly suppressed. People begin to look the other way. After a while, people become indifferent.

Yet courage can't become extinct altogether. Because it's a trait that was built into the human organism through countless generations of evolution, when our ancestors were forced to do battle with the Ice Age and saber-toothed tigers. Courage is there, in each of us. A little dormant, perhaps, through years of slumber—but it's there. And it can be brought out again and developed—*if* the individual wants it so.

How do you develop courage? Just as you would any other trait: First you have to want to acquire that trait. Then you have to practice it.

As an example, say a soldier is walking across a minefield, but he doesn't know it's a minefield. He thinks he's walking across a meadow. Is he exhibiting courage? No. (Well . . . unless he happens to have agoraphobia . . .) But if the soldier knows there are mines there and he still goes, despite the danger, because that's what he has to do—well, that takes a lot of courage.

Fortunately, few of us are called upon to walk a minefield in our daily lives. Yet personal courage is just as important for us as it is for the soldier.

But we also have to know how to apply it, because, like any other trait, it can be misdirected and misused. Take, for example, the white-knuckle flier. A person who goes on a plane trip, fearfully holding on to himself, hour after hour, is certainly showing courage—but it's the wrong kind. It's not necessary—because there's a better way.

As Dr. Weekes writes: "Recovery is not built on knowing you had the courage to board the bus and sit through hell with clenched teeth . . . recovery lies in learning to sit in the bus with the right attitude."

- When your fight-or-flight instinct is aroused and you get that urge to run away—*but* you know that feeling is only temporary and that the best way to handle it is to relax and not run;
- When you start those what-if thoughts—*but* you know you should be turning all those what-ifs into a cheerful "so what";
- When you really want to go somewhere and that little voice starts to say, "What if I go there and get a panic attack and make a fool of myself in front of all those people?"— *but* you know you should answer, "The hell with that . . . who cares?"—and you go anyway . . .

That's showing courage!

Forgiveness

Forgiveness means letting go of the hurts of the past. It means forgiving others for some of their mistakes, their shortcomings. But most importantly, it means forgiving yourself. For not getting well sooner. For not being strong enough, brave enough, or smart enough. A true spirit of forgiveness will wash away much of the suffering and pain.

Hope

Hope is a very powerful emotion. It's one of the strongest positive emotions we have. Even love, which we think of as another powerful emotion, has undertones of hope in it. When we're in love, we look at another person and see ourselves already happy, already walking off together into a glorious future. So—when you stop and think about it—it's really hope—not so much the immediate feelings of admiration and tenderness—that makes falling in love such a beautiful experience for us. Hope is what gives our inner chemistry that strong boost—like a shot of amphetamines. And suddenly everything in the world becomes marvelous and bright.

We used the phrase, "like a shot of amphetamines." But it's more than just a metaphor. It happens to be true. A chemical very much like the amphetamines is released in the brain—and it's this chemical (actually, a combination of chemicals) that gives us that high when we're in love, when we're hopeful.

So science again is reaffirming what we've known all along: that things like hope, love, trust and faith are something real and solid, not just ethereal things-of-the-mind. These emotions can and should be evoked as often as possible, so that the body's chemistry can correct itself and re-create that harmony between the stress chemicals and the good chemicals we spoke about earlier.

Unfortunately, in our society, things like hope, courage, faith, and trust—in other words, the spiritual values—are not stressed enough. They're not part of everyday life. In fact, just the opposite is true: The negative is what you hear most in the media—alcoholism, drug abuse, crime, wars.

No, we cannot control the outside world. But we do have some measure of control about what goes on in our own minds—not by stifling information and saying, "Oh, I mustn't think about it" (you know by now that's not the way), but by filling your life with music, art, loving, dance, friends—and all the beautiful things you want to happen to you. If you take these into your life, if you think about these things and make them a part of your daily habits, they'll exert an effect on your life. So, the positive input will replace or neutralize some of the negative input. And more of the healing process will take place.

How do you encourage your body to produce more of these chemicals? By putting yourself—bodily—into situations where such emotions can more easily be generated.

You do this by setting your life up so that you maximize the opportunities your body has to manufacture these good chemicals. When you exercise, you do that; when you eat good foods, you do that; when you balance your work with play, you do that; when you're in the company of good friends, you do that—and so on. You may not be able to control everything, but you can set things up so the chances of a successful outcome will be very high.

For example, if feelings of faith and trust can be evoked by hearing a Sunday sermon, by all means, go to church. If feelings of hope can be fanned by reading inspiring books, by all means, read inspiring books. If you get a lift when friends come over to sit and chat, by all means, make your home inviting and pleasant—so people will want to come over and visit you. This is your responsibility to yourself.

But do faith and trust come first—and then does the body start making the good chemicals? Or is it the other way around? I think this is a little like the chicken-or-the-egg question. It doesn't matter much which comes first. The pattern is a circular one anyhow.

Faith

Faith can take many forms. It can be interpreted by each of us according to our own experience, our own background and belief.

A professor once told me that he thought trusting your body and mind meant "allowing yourself to be restored by your own inner mechanisms." I liked that answer. After all, when a doctor treats a person, what he does is to adjust or arrange favorable circumstances so that the body's own ability to heal itself can take over. Isn't this how the doctor treats a broken leg? All he does is align the bones the right way—and nature takes care of the rest. The doctor himself doesn't knit the bones together. The inner mechanisms do that. Machines can't repair themselves, but our bodies and minds can. Exactly how this works is beyond our understanding. Yet our job is to trust this life-force within. And as we do, we reaffirm our faith.

We're not talking here in a strictly religious sense— one need not be a religious person in order to experience faith. Even a scientist, who happens to be an aetheist, must operate from the vantage point of faith: He knows that when he mixes several chemicals together, they will always yield the same compound; that the stars are there even if he can't see them; that the scientific principles he discovers today will still hold true tomorrow.

But we also have to have more faith in our bodies, in our minds, in our cells. If you haven't walked down Main Street, or been to the center of your town in years, it requires a leap of faith to open the door—and walk out.

Yes, it's sometimes difficult to trust, to have faith. But it's even more difficult without it.

Naturally, we're not presuming to tell you what to believe in. That's between you and your conscience, as they say. What we are suggesting is that a belief in something of value, something greater than yourself (or your fear), is an essential component in the development of a serene and tranquil attitude.

PART III

Preparing for Adventure

CHAPTER 12

Making Your Trip More Enjoyable

"Life is either a daring adventure—or it is nothing."

—*Helen Keller*

Motivation

ONE OF OUR clients once told me after she had been in the PASS-Group program for two-and-half months, that she "can now go all over, except—," and she mentioned the name of the next town. I asked, "What's in the next town?" And she said, "My mother-in-law lives there." I asked, "Do you want to visit your mother-in-law?" She said, "No."

So, motivation is the key that can open up many doors. Here is an example. One of our clients, Alice (whose story is included in this book), lives in Vermont. Her greatest wish was to be able to come to Brooklyn to visit her family. I (SAS) was her counselor and I also happened to live in Brooklyn.

Alice was in the program just about the time of the Brooklyn Bridge Centennial celebration. At one point in our sessions, I felt she was ready to make the trip—and I told her so. Her first reaction was, "Oh, no—not me, not now. I'm not ready yet." But I knew she was. So I began sending her leaflets about the celebration (describing Brooklyn in such glowing terms). That was to get her to build up an appetite, to become more mentally ready to go. And it worked. Each time she demurred a little less. Then Alice wrote a letter to her family in Brooklyn, telling them that maybe—just maybe—she might be coming to see them. Well, letters flew back and forth; everyone became excited about Alice's visit. And this momentum just picked up its own rhythm, and culminated in a wonderful adventure. Not only for Alice, but for her family as well.

If you're finding it difficult to venture out, to get going, you're probably using the wrong approach. You probably daydream of a Magic Day, when you'll wake up one morning and find you're suddenly transformed into a person with a desire to go to such-and-such a place. Well, it's a nice dream. The only problem is—that's not the way it happens.

Inertia, the wish to let things remain the way they are, is a very powerful force in our lives. It's as true with people as it is with physics. A person would much prefer NOT to change unless there's a strong force—most often an outside force—that *pulls* him away from the status quo; that *draws* him away from A to B because he wants to be at Point B.

If you want to do something and there is no "outside force" to compel you, then you have to create it yourself. You have to find, in the place you want to go, a sort of magnet that will draw you there; lure you; beg you to come!

Sure, it's easy to just sit back and daydream, "Yes, some day I'll do such-and-such." But if the wish is too vague and fuzzy, then, of course, it won't work. Napoleon Hill, the well-known author, understood this perfectly. "There is a difference," he said, "between wishing for a thing and being ready to receive it. No one is ready for a thing," he added, "until he believes he can acquire it. Until he has a burning desire for it. The state of mind cannot be merely hope or wish."

If you can't get going on your own, you may mistakenly consider yourself weak. Or think you have no willpower. But this isn't fair to you. You're not being weak. You're just using your mental resources incorrectly; you're working with the wrong set of tools. You have to understand that the mind needs a goal, something to draw towards a goal; otherwise, it doesn't budge.

So, in order to change and start moving, you have to put a carrot in front of the donkey.

If you don't have a carrot, you have to scrounge around until you find one. Because it's up to you to arrange the circumstances that will allow this to happen. If you don't do it, Life does it for you. But you have to wait, in that case. And who knows how long?

It reminds me of a woman I once knew. She absolutely refused to travel beyond her limit, which was a 100-mile radius from her Brooklyn home. When her husband would suggest a trip to another city, she'd measure the distance on the map—and if it was, say 102 miles, she wouldn't go. She told me she was that way ever since she was a girl. And when her son moved to another state, she wanted very much to visit him—but she couldn't go; it was too far. She had lost her husband some years before, and she lived near a sister to whom she was very close. But eventually the sister and her husband moved to California. It was only then that she finally decided to ignore her 100-mile limit. And for the first time in her life, at age seventy, she boarded a plane and flew to California.

So you see how motivation works? Without a lure, without a bait—something to coax you, to make you want to do it—nothing gets done. You can say from here until tomorrow, "Oh, how I'd love to go to such-and-such a place," but you won't go there unless you find the magnet that will draw you there.

So, the next time you plan your trip, make it interesting, exciting. Plan to do something that you really enjoy. This will give you the necessary impetus to get you out of the house.

Pleasurable Tie-ins

The aim is to build up new and pleasurable associations with the once-dreaded fear-place. By tying in something pleasant with a formerly unpleasant task that must be done, you're establishing a much less formidable situation. It's almost as if the two—the plus and the minus—cancel each other out, and the result is a neutral acceptance, which may later turn out to be a real pleasure.

Here are some examples of how little pleasures can ease big burdens:

One woman in the program ties in her love of opera with her fear of driving. She keeps cassette tapes of her favorite operas in the car, and listens as she drives. A young woman who used to dread waiting in line at the supermarket now picks up a magazine at the checkout counter and reads happily about Elizabeth Taylor's newest husband while waiting for her "next." One woman who used to worry about standing on an open platform to wait for her train now buys an evening paper to make her wait more pleasurable. Another young lady, whose fear was elevators, memorizes jokes in the elevator from little index cards she carries with her. She's well on her way to becoming the life of the party with her repertoire of jokes! One woman brings her knitting along. When I (SAS) go on extended trips, I also like to bring along some handwork to do. On one trip, I brought along my crocheting and a little bag of many-colored yarn. I can still remember how comforting this was to me, to look at all the exciting colors and to design the placing of these granny squares. I still enjoy, years later, the blanket I made then.

One of our clients, a woman who lives in a very small town, had to drive her sister to the nearest large city to undergo a medical procedure. The hospital was about a hundred miles away. She was very nervous about that long trip. I advised her to prepare beforehand—three topics of conversation for the car ride, based on some childhood experiences. The topics I suggested were: "My Happiest Childhood Memory," "An Embarrassing Experience," and "The Time We Put Something Over On—." She told me afterward that the long drive turned out to be a very pleasant experience (and this despite the seriousness of the situation itself). The woman and her sister felt so much closer to each other, she said, sharing and remembering childhood experiences. They even stopped off on the way back to visit a country fair. And no panic attacks!

Being called on to speak in public used to be one of my (SAS) biggest fears. No, not fears—terrors! I couldn't address more than three people without feeling faint. But it wasn't until I tied in public speaking with my interest in poetry that things really began to change. I always enjoyed poetry; I had written and collected poems since the age of twelve. I joined a poetry workshop a few years ago; we had to get up in front of the class to read our poems. I've found such experiences to be so pleasurable, I can now do this without a trace of my former audience fear. I learned that experience—coupled with something pleasant—can be the best teacher.

So you see, you don't have to grit your teeth and bear it. There are so many ways to make your trips or experiences enjoyable!

Once, when I was talking to a client who was planning her first trip downtown, she said to me, "Never mind about making the trip more enjoyable—I'd be satisfied just to get there!" And I answered, "But that's the whole point! It has to be made more enjoyable if you want to get there."

You have to dangle a carrot in order to move the cart!

All at Once

Some years ago, an ad appeared in several women's magazines, picturing a kitchen sink with a stack of dirty dishes that reached the ceiling. A horrified housewife was surveying the mess. I forgot what it advertised, but the caption read something like this: "How would you like to wash a year's dirty dishes all at once?" Yet some people want to be able to do just that! They want to do *all* their work at once; they want to see the *whole* road they're traveling *all* at once; they want to have everything *now*, *all* at once!

Maralyn L. Teare writes, "I observed, while working with phobic people, that there is a direct correlation between length of gaze and symptom level. What this means is: The farther the person looks into the distance and the more that is consumed visually, the higher the symptom level." Sight, she points out, is our chief sense and provides us with more environmental information than any of our other senses. Therefore, it's the most important single factor in keeping the brain busy. In addition, looking ahead implies contemplating the future: "What will happen when I'm at Point A?"

When I (SAS) was first learning to drive, I was overwhelmed by the traffic around me. I looked at all the cars coming from the other side and wondered about a head-on collision: What if one of those cars crossed over to my lane? My driving instructor told me to concentrate on my own lane, to watch the space in front of me, and to think about where I was going. In other words, to mind my own business and not try to see all the roads at once!

When I did that, my driving improved. When you limit your attention to the task in front of you and stop trying to see everything—past, present, and future—all at once, your level of nervousness goes down.

Does this mean you shouldn't plan? Of course not. You *plan* the *overall* setting; then you relax, and direct your attention to what's at hand.

Testing, Testing

Many people when they first venture out to new places or try new things will go with the mental attitude of testing themselves: "How am I doing?" (New York's Mayor Koch says it sort of jokingly—but these people are serious.)

We think this is the wrong attitude, really. Think back when you were in school. Remember test day? How everyone was so nervous? So you're putting an extra burden on yourself when you consider the things you do as a test. It conjures up that old critical Self again, the one who always watches you with such a grim expression.

It can throw a damper on any experimentation or innovation you might want to try.

Think of it, rather, in these terms: You've already learned to use a number of tools or techniques. Take one of the 7 steps, for example: imagination. You can fantasize. You can pretend you're someone else—or somewhere else. When you make the situation different and better, you lessen the impact of the experience. You can do the QR. You can allow gravity to tug at your sleeves and pull at your muscles, to relax them. You can slow down and breathe diaphragmatically. Instead of thinking of the coming adventure as a test, pretend you're the doctor—a surgeon—with a nurse standing by, holding a trayful of instruments (tools) and *you* select whatever tool you need to carry out your assignment.

This mind-set will help you think about all the knowledge you've acquired, all the things you can do. Isn't it better to see the situation you're about to encounter as a place to play with your newfound tools—as an opportunity to experiment with them?

If you haven't done something in a while—or if you're doing something for the first time, of course you're going to feel "strange" or a bit apprehensive. That's only normal. (I remember even after recovering from the flu and going out "for the first time," it would feel strange the first day just being outdoors again.) So give yourself time to get adjusted.

A Trip to the Beach

It may take a little planning to prepare for a trip the right way, but the results are well worth it.

Here, for example, is what one client told us:

My goal, when I started the PASS program, was to be able to truly enjoy a vacation with my family. So I'm going to tell you what happened this time when we went on vacation.

I was always terribly afraid of bridges (among many other things!) because I'd always get a panic attack whenever I crossed a bridge. I used to worry all the time: What if I get stuck there and can't leave? Anyhow, my family wanted very much to go to the beach (another place for panicking). But in order to get there, we had to cross a very long bridge.

We left on a Friday, about 4:30 or so in the afternoon. There was myself, my husband, my two children—and each of the kids brought along a friend. We went in two cars; it was a four-hour drive. The thing that had really been worrying me about this trip was the fact that this was my first big trip since I joined the program. So it was like the first time out. Then, there was that bridge (a *drawbridge*, yet!).

I had prepared for it exactly as the program suggested. I looked up material about the bridge in the encyclopedia, and I began to think of it in a factual way rather than in an emotional way. I began to replace myths with facts. I used to worry about lights on the bridge: What if it turned red and we had to stop? But I realized there's a reason for the light. The bridge has to open up so a big ship can go through. So you just have to wait there patiently until it's your turn to go. I kept that in the back of my mind. And I really started to feel calmer when I would think about it.

Until the day of the trip! Then, all these negative things were just assaulting my mind. And it was then that everything was blown out of proportion—like the bridge was going to be a million miles long! But, anyway, I packed the food; we piled into the car, and took off.

It was dark, so I couldn't do any knitting or reading. I just "acted as if." I was doing all the right things outwardly—or inwardly, I don't know which—but I wasn't totally relaxed all the time. Intermittently, I kept hearing in my mind the relaxation tape and then I'd feel waves of relaxation going through me. And so I stayed pretty relaxed. I didn't at any time lose control as far as getting a panic attack, but I wasn't as totally relaxed as I would have been, sitting at home. I just continued to "act as if," going through the motions, and doing all the right things I knew I should be doing. Yet, from time to time, I'd be thinking: Bridge—bridge—bridge.

Well, we finally reached the bridge. So, here's the bridge in view, and here we are, traveling right up to it. And I'm thinking, "Oh, there's the bridge!" Then, we came on to the bridge, and I didn't have any panic at all! It was so nice—that bridge was beautiful! I looked down at the water and I just loved it! When we got off, I wanted to go on that bridge again! That was the best time I ever had. I was thrilled and amazed. But I was also proud of myself because, at the same time, I had all those other past experiences to compare it with. And here I was—I looked over the ocean, down near the bridge, and I said to myself, "Gosh, isn't this the most beautiful, breathtaking sight?" Whereas before, I used to hold on to the car, gritting my teeth and being panicky all the way over any sort of bridge, even a small one.

As I told my husband afterward, that was a really big hurdle out of my way. And it was the first time in my whole life that I enjoyed the beach. Before, the openness and the sound of the waves—they were sort of "outside" things, while my own mind felt sort of dark and scary. (I don't know how else to explain it.) So I never enjoyed the beach. But this time it was totally different: I loved it! In fact, the whole experience was great! Coming back on the bridge, I felt the same thrill and happy excitement as before. So I think I'm just doing great!

Here, in summary, are ways to help make your trip more enjoyable:

1. Have a definite, pleasant destination. Don't just go for the sake of going . . . or to test yourself. (Very few so-called normal people would relish the thought of going out without a specific destination or purpose.) So, visit a friend . . . go to the library . . . browse around a card shop . . . buy something, etc.

2. If at all possible, have a friend meet you at your destination or at a halfway point, to complete the trip together. If that's not possible, call up a friend before you leave the house *and* when you get to your destination. Make it a shared experience!

3. By all means, *plan* your overall trip before you start. But also make allowances for the unexpected. Look forward to small delights: colors, sounds, experiences. It'll make your trip far more interest-

ing than if you try to plan each little detail in advance (it never quite works out that way, anyhow).

4. Realize this: The chances of something bad happening on this very trip are—statistically speaking—very, very slim indeed! So why spoil your trip with unnecessary worry?

5. Have an enjoyable errand to do. Example: if you're going visiting, bring along a small gift. If you're going to a store, buy a little something. If you're going for a walk, be prepared (mentally) to enjoy the street scene, gardens, whatever.

6. Make sure you're as well or appropriately dressed as possible. Wear something new if you can. It'll give you a lift. Women should wear makeup.

7. Bring along some food (complex carbohydrate plus protein). Don't rely on what's out there (otherwise, you'll probably end up with a chocolate bar).

8. Greet neighbors with cheerfulness and enthusiasm. Get into a positive social mood (put on an act, if you have to!) Smile—or better yet, laugh—before you even open the door.

9. If it wouldn't make you feel foolish, it's quite all right to take along a security blanket or good luck charm—a letter, medallion, penny, etc. (But don't choose overt props that you can hide behind—like an umbrella or dark glasses.)

10. If you seem to have a lot of nervous energy ready to pounce out of you, think of it as excitement, which it is, rather than nervousness. Words can have strong positive or negative connotations. "Nervousness" is such a negative word, "excitement," a positive one. So you might as well express your feelings in a positive way.

Remember: Everyone experiences a heightened sense of excitement when they do something new. Many people find this excitement highly pleasurable—that's why they're always eager to try something new, to visit new places. So don't become unduly concerned if you're experiencing more excitement than usual. It's perfectly normal.

11. Have something enjoyable to do during the trip. Example: If you're on a bus, read, crochet, solve a crossword puzzle, study faces, write a poem, etc. If you're out walking, admire the gardens on the way. Whenever possible, stop to chat with someone. Be friendly.

12. See yourself as very much a part of the Universe, a product of our planet Earth. Feel that sense of connectedness with all living things. Know that we have common roots that reach far, far back in time.

13. Remember, as a child, watching the moon from a moving car? How it seemed to move along with you wherever you went? Make yourself the center of your little world, pulling everything along with you wherever you go. "Wherever I go, that's where I am," says Dr. Wayne Dyer.

14. As you walk (or sit in a car) *let go* of all muscles not in use. Make those muscles as slack as possible. Even when they seem quite relaxed, make them even more "floppy."

15. As soon as you begin to experience more excitement than is comfortable for you, do the QR.

16. Don't go jumping too far ahead of yourself. Don't try to see every aspect of the journey all at once. Break it up into one baby step at a time. You go to Point B, then to C, then to D, and so on.

17. For this trip only: Don't be such a perfectionist. Whatever happens, "Let it happen." Make up your mind to enjoy it all.

18. And, perhaps the most important point of all: Act *as if* you're already cured.

CHAPTER 13

Anticipatory Anxiety

> "If I'm not nervous before a show, I
> know I'm not going to be at my best
> that night."
>
> —*Jack Benny*

SOMETIMES A STATE of "anticipatory anxiety," or excitement, is deliberately sought. Think of the Indian war dances before a battle. Or the African jungle drums before a hunt. All this is an attempt to rev up the system physically and get the warriors ready.

But the way some people talk (with dread) about anticipatory anxiety, you'd think it was the name of a new disease!

Whenever *anyone* faces an important event—for you, it may be going to the supermarket, for someone else, it may be giving a lecture or looking for a job—there's bound to be a higher level of brain activity and neural excitation than if he's relaxing in an armchair.

Some excited anticipation before an important performance is entirely normal, especially when a person believes that the particular act he is about to perform will have an effect on his whole future. Even seasoned actors and actresses experience some butterflies before a performance.

There's certainly nothing unusual about that. These people are putting themselves on the line. The acts they'll soon be performing are important to them. So the nervous system has to build up momentum for a good performance. It only becomes a problem when you worry about this too much.

I (SSJ) was once watching a race on TV and the camera zoomed in on the runners. I could actually see the muscle tension in the legs as the runners crouched in position, waiting for the race to begin. Their muscles were quivering. But once that shot was fired, all their tremendous pent-up energy was suddenly released. It's liked a coiled-up spring that's suddenly let go. The analogy is apt because muscle fibers (if you were to view them under a microscope) actually coil up and shorten when they're held in a state of anticipation. That's to prepare the body for action. But once the action is taken, the tension diminishes. The muscle fibers lengthen and become stretched out again.

If you own a cat, watch him the next time he's preparing to attack. His whole body fairly ripples from the strain. Those muscles he'll be using are coiling up, shortening, getting wound up for the leap.

But is the runner concerned or worried because his muscles quiver before a race? Is your cat concerned because his tail twitches? No, of course not. They're not observing themselves. Their minds are focused only on the activity they intend to perform. Notice I didn't say "about to perform" but "intend to perform." In other words, they are doing this willingly and with purpose. They're not adding more tension by observing themselves and berating themselves because they're nervous.

But what can you do if your nervous system is a bit too revved up for comfort?

You can always tone it down by changing your perception of the situation. You can minimize its importance. You can pretend (or really believe, if you can) that the event about to take place is not as earth-shattering as it seems, that in the long run it's of little significance in your life. You can lessen the importance of the event by *choosing* to see it this way. You can remind yourself that in the cosmic scheme of things, this particular event ranks pretty low, that it's no big deal. (It's the old "sour grapes" mechanism.)

This self-dialogue will effectively take the edge off the panic. Why? Because if you tell yourself there's no race, nothing worth fighting for, then there's no point in getting all revved up, is there?

When I (SAS) had my first radio interview about PASS-Group, I remember on the way to the studio saying things like this to myself: "It's just a small radio station. Not many people listen, and most people aren't interested anyway. And those who do listen, they're just people. Like me. So it's no big deal really. Even if I say something real stupid, so what?"

A story we mentioned earlier also illustrates this maneuver. Dr. Sehnert, while waiting backstage for his cue to go on, knew this was not the moment to be telling himself, "Hey, wow! I'll soon be on the world-famous *Tonight Show* that's being broadcast nationwide. Soon millions of people will be looking at me. I better be good, I mustn't fluff it, otherwise I'll never be able to face my friends again." He started down that path, but he caught himself in time. He told himself something like this: "Hey, Johnny's just another guy from Nebraska. I'll just talk to him, man to man." Dr. Sehnert looked at the experience from a totally different angle—and it worked.

You have two very useful tools to work with. First, to realize that your nervous system is just behaving normally when it gets excited before an important event. And second, to know that you can lower your excitement at will by changing your perception about the situation.

Take Your Time

Many panic attack sufferers are very impatient. They want to get more and more done before some (often imaginary) deadline. They want to rush time, speed the river along, faster, faster. If they're out, they're always looking at the clock, counting the minutes till they can leave and run back home. When they're home, they want to be instantly cured—so they can rush out again. No wonder Dr. Weekes has, as one of her basic principles, the admonition to "let time pass."

I (SAS) remember once, long ago, being on a bus in Manhattan. I was already late for an appointment and the bus was stuck in heavy traffic. Cars and taxis were honking their horns; there was confusion all around; and my bus was not moving. I was very impatient. I wanted the bus to go—*now*. I clearly remember looking down at my hands. I had grabbed the seat in front of me and was straining to "push" the bus from the inside! At least I had the wits to realize what I was doing, and I stopped. Now, whenever I find myself in any vehicle (or in any situation beyond my control), I simply relax and let the driver take over. I don't "assist" anymore.

What can you do to counteract this rush-rush tendency? First of all, and this is an obvious first step, you have to allow plenty of time to prepare things so you don't have to rush. (For instance, in the example I gave above, I could have left the house much earlier.)

Secondly, there's the temptation to do everything at once. So you just have to repeat to yourself firmly, "I'll only do one thing at a time." And do it that way.

Another very effective measure is this: Stop where you are and begin to do everything in s-l-o-w motion. Many people have a bad habit of rushing around the house just before they leave, checking to see if they left the gas on, looking for their keys, or their sweater. So all you do is switch to slow motion. If you consistently move with an exaggerated slow action, that will soon become a signal to you, an automatic response, to slow down.

Here's what one of our clients told us:

> Every morning, my son has to be in school by 12:30. So you'd think I had plenty of time to get ready and I wouldn't have to rush. But I always used to be what I'd call a last minute person. As the time would draw near when I had to take my son to school, I'd start rushing around the house like a maniac, looking for my key, looking for his jacket, and I'd get to school all tense and jittery.
>
> But now it's so different—since my counselor told me about this slow-motion technique. I just go around and do what I have to do—but slowly. Everything gets done. I don't feel rushed. My son is on time. And when I get to school I'm calm and I talk with the other mothers. That rush-rush feeling is gone, and my days are a lot easier now!

Those Constant What-ifs

Constant what-iffing seems to be the trademark of the panic attack sufferer!

And yet—such thinking isn't bad—by itself. After all, all our inventions, our great ideas in the arts, in the sciences, must have started with this one basic question: "What if it works like this . . . ?" Or: "What if I do this differently . . . ?" That's what Edison did, didn't he? He must have asked himself thousands of times: "What if I use this material as a filament instead of that?" And then there was light! (Can you just picture Colonel Sanders asking himself, "What if ah make up a batch of Mother's chicken recipe and sell it?" Or Picasso asking himself, "Hm-m. What if I paint three eyes instead of two?")

So, what-if questions and looking ahead can be tremendously useful and appropriate—in their place. But if all your questions are: "What if I go there and get into an accident?" "What if I didn't shut the gas and the house explodes?" or: "What if I go there and get a panic attack?"—you've simply placed all your creative energy into one basket—and the wrong basket, at that!

You have a questioning, think-ahead mind. You're evidently creative. Many people we've known through our program write poetry, or books. They paint, do needlework, or woodwork. We are seeing, I think, a far greater percentage of artistic people than could be accounted for on a statistical basis. But you have taken these wonderful, God-given gifts—and put them to wrong use. You've been creating colorful pictures of catastrophes wherever you go. It's time you took your creative imagination and turned it around—and let it work *for* you instead of against you!

Answering Those What-ifs

Never be afraid to face your what-ifs, and to answer them in kind.

Some people, in an attempt to rid themselves of the

constantly tormenting question, what-if, make the mistake of trying to turn off all such thoughts by refusing to think about them. Whenever such a thought comes sneaking around, they become alarmed and do their best to squelch that thought—without even examining it. (Some will even have a rubber band tied to their wrist, so they can snap it—and punish themselves—whenever a what-if thought comes along!)

But this method is self-defeating. It only makes the thought cling to you more and more. You always have to feel free to look at your own thoughts and feelings—no matter what they are. This is not to say, of course, that you should constantly analyze your thoughts—or take your mental temperature all the time, so to speak. ("Now, what I am feeling right now?"; "What do I feel like doing?") Being overly concerned about transient moods or paying too much attention to fleeting emotions is not such a great idea, either. But when a serious what-if question comes to your mind, you don't have to be afraid to examine it and answer it.

A few examples come to mind: An out-of-town guest and I (SAS) were traveling by subway. At one point, the subway became an elevated line and as we looked out the window, my friend noted a curve ahead, on the line. She started to get very worried for fear the train wouldn't make the curve. She had never been on an elevated before, and the thought—naturally enough—occurred to her: "What if the train falls down?" I reassured her by telling her that this elevated line was built long before I was born and that this very train and other trains like it had been making daily trips for many, many years without mishap. Therefore, the chance of the train falling down within the next few minutes was very, very remote indeed. She immediately became calm again.

One client, who uses the subway to go to work, became fearful whenever the train stopped between stations; most of his panic attacks would occur during those times. At some level, he was seeing the halted train as a sign of great danger ("Uh-oh, now there's trouble—something must have happened"). So, of course, his sentry reacted—(Why shouldn't it?). But after we talked about it, he began to see the situation more realistically and in a different way.

I pointed out that there are traffic signals in a subway tunnel, just as there are in the streets. (Of course, he knew this; it just didn't register at the time.) When there is a train just ahead, I said, your train has to stop in order to avoid a collision. The motorman must obey the signals and stop as a safety measure. (Now the halted train becomes associated with safety rather than with danger.) I also suggested to my client that he look around him and watch the other passengers during one of these train stops. I've been riding the subways for years and have always observed how nervous people get whenever the train stops between stations—especially if it's a long stop. People start to cough, to fidget, to look around with worried expressions. They're literally left in the dark. (In fact, so many people complained about this problem that the transit authority finally installed speakers in the cars so the motormen could announce, during stops, the reason for the halt and, if necessary, give instructions.) I was able to convince this man that he wasn't the only one; that there was no shame about being afraid or uneasy.

So, you see, a realistic appraisal of the situation can be as important a tool as fantasy. As this man began to view the situation in a different light, he was able to turn the situation around. The panic attacks in the train subsided and he is now able to ride the subway quite comfortably, without becoming unduly alarmed about a halted train.

Another instance: a former client was traveling by car along an unfamiliar mountain road at night. He was alone. At one point he felt very tense and uncomfortable. But he used a relaxation technique and the moment passed. Later, however, he was quite disturbed by what he imagined was a return of the panic attacks that he used to experience. Evidently, this what-if thought must have crossed his mind as he drove: "What if my car tumbles over the cliff?" It's a natural thought that any driver might have. By being aware of the danger, one drives more carefully. (That's the purpose of fear, isn't it?) So, instead of trying to silence that thought, he might have answered it: "Look, I'm a good driver—and I'm careful. I'm not going too fast. And I've traveled unfamiliar roads before—and I got through all right. So I'm pretty safe."

The only way you can dispel those bad what-ifs is by confronting them—and answering them. How do you answer them? That depends on the situation. Most of them can be dismissed by just putting the word "so" in front of the sentence you tell yourself: "So what if I go there and get a panic attack?" (Big, hairy deal . . . !) Others require logic and reason (as in the above-mentioned illustrations).

Here are some other useful counterquestions: "What are the chances of such-and-such happening?" Or: "What is the worst that can possibly happen?"

And sometimes you just have to say to yourself: "I'm going to face that with courage."

The Fear of Being Nervous

Many people get so upset when they become nervous. I think that, as human beings, we're entitled to be nervous on occasion—without making a federal case out of it. Years ago, there was a character in the Dick Tracy comic strip called Fearless Fosdick. He "didn't have a nerve in his body." But he was a made-up character. Real flesh-and-blood people are nervous sometimes. And they do feel frightened at times. But—so what? A little excitement now and then never hurt anyone.

Once you admit that it's OK to be nervous (especially when there's something to be nervous about!), the paradox, of course, is that this admission usually reduces the level of nervousness.

And you can do another thing: As we pointed out before, you can convert your nervousness into enthusiasm—and enjoy the excitement of being aware and alive.

A certain story comes to mind. I (SAS) remember one of my clients, a young man of twenty, who had suffered from agoraphobia for several years and had been homebound for several months when he started this program. But once he was able to go out again, naturally enough, he wanted to start dating. He knew he'd be nervous on his first date, and he was afraid that his nervousness would turn into panic attacks again. I advised him to convert that excess nervous energy into enthusiasm—for his date. To focus all his attention on her, not on himself—and to make her feel she was the "prettiest girl in the world."

Well, it worked like a charm. I understand he became immensely popular with the girls by applying this method. (And the fact that he also happened to be tall, dark, and handsome didn't hurt any either—I saw him; he came to visit me one day.)

By the way, there's a rather novel twist to this story: About six months later, he called me again, just to say hello. It seems he found a job in Manhattan and was living it up in an apartment he shared with friends in Greenwich Village. He told me there was lots of partying going on—often the parties lasted till dawn—and that he wasn't exactly following his diet any more. The panic attacks were coming back, he said. "But," he added, "I've never had so much fun in my life! If panic attacks are the price I have to pay, well, that's it, then. I'll pay." I told him, "Listen—who am I to quarrel with you? If it's OK with you, it's certainly OK with me." He felt in control, you see. He knew what they were; he knew what would make them go away—*if* he chose to do so. And he wasn't worried about them.

Watching Your Self

The mind is meant to be used as an instrument to examine the outside world, to reflect, perhaps, on the inner world, in a philosophical sense, and to somehow bring them together in harmony. The mind was not designed for constant introspection, constant self-analysis, self-absorption. If you do this, you're not using your body/mind correctly—the way nature intended. Just as a stomach is not supposed to digest itself, only what's put into it—so a mind has to be directed "out there" and not always inwardly, watching your Self all the time.

If you know someone is watching you all the time, doesn't that make you a little uneasy? Being observed by anybody—including your own Self—can make a person so self-conscious that it would be hard to do anything right. Try this: Walk across a room and be aware each second of how you move your arms, how you bend your right knee, at what angle, how you bend your left knee, and so on. A person watching you walk like that would think you're a wooden soldier. Being so self-conscious (which, literally, means conscious of your Self) tends to jam the machinery. Your body can't operate smoothly.

There's a little anecdote about a mediocre tennis player who always beat his opponents, who were much better players. Someone asked him, "How in the world did you ever manage to beat so-and-so?" He replied, "Simple. All I did was ask him: 'Do you take a breath before or after you serve?' "

When you go out, you're not supposed to be thinking about how your legs move, how you're feeling, whether you're breathing the right way—or things like that. This intense concentration with your Self can only bring on the very thing you *don't* want to happen.

So, when you go somewhere—switch to automatic; let your mind wander on the other matters (ideas, letter-writing, thinking things out, whatever). In other words, "*you*" get out of the way.

CHAPTER 14

Dealing with the Unknown

On this subject, my adopted mottos
are "Don't worry until you have to,"
and "One door closes, another door
opens."

SAS

MANY PEOPLE HAVE the mistaken notion that being cured
means just going out into the world willy-nilly, wander-
ing about here and there without feeling anything but a
carefree state of freedom. What a lot of cat-fat! I don't
know why this vagabond myth is so widespread, but it is.

To many people who suffer from panic attacks, there
seems to be a wide chasm between the sick and the well.
But it really isn't so. What normal person just picks
himself up and hops on a train (or plane) and heads for
who knows where? Do you know anyone who says to
himself, "Hm, let's see . . . today's Sunday. I think I'll
take a flight down to Pickleville, Arkansas—just to see
what it's like?" Do you know anyone like that? (Neither
do I.) Everyone is more comfortable with the known, the
familiar—and somewhat leery of the unknown. That's
just how the human organism is wired.

You can observe this all around you. At a meeting, for
instance, nine times out of ten, people will choose the
same chair they had the last time. We all have our little
daily habits related to dressing, eating, sleeping. Change
is difficult for everyone—but, naturally, in varying degrees. But even those who, by any standards, are considered hardy and adventurous still have the same need for
the familiar, the known. Columbus knew where he was
going. Or thought he knew. I'm sure he plotted and
charted his journey on the maps of his day. The explor-

ers who went to the Poles knew where they were going; they made provisions against the cold—and learned whatever was knowable about the regions they were going into.

Watch a small child beginning to explore his environment. He stands on his little two feet, takes a few steps forward, pokes little fingers at something strange on the table, tests the table by touching it, slapping it, then looks back to Mama for approval. If she nods and smiles, the baby goes on with his exploring—testing, taking little steps, always coming back to safe ground, then trying again. And this pattern is repeated throughout life: looking ahead, trying to understand, to conquer the unknown little by little; testing it, bringing it slowly into the known world. Nobody just rides off into the unknown without a plan or purpose.

I remember when I (SAS) embarked on a program to unmask the unknown. I went to visit Kennedy Airport in New York City. I talked to people waiting on line for tickets . . . passengers who just arrived . . . porters . . . anyone I could grab hold of. And most people told me—yes, they, too, were afraid to fly the first time. But now, they said, "it's like sitting in your living room." I went to the observation deck and watched for hours, planes taking off and landing. (The grace of those huge metal birds was unbelievable!)

Not only did I go to the airport, but I read as much as I could about the history of aviation and the principles of aerodynamics. When the day finally came and I walked into that plane, I acted as if I were a seasoned traveler. There were many babies on that plane. I pretended (inside myself) that I was a baby, too—being taken by my mommy on the plane. The trip itself was fantastic! (All that homework paid off.) I watched the sun come up at 3 A.M. by my watch. I looked down and, mirrorlike, saw pink-and-blue clouds. I thought: How many men in countless ages must have yearned to fly. I remember reading a story about the Greek who ordered huge wings to be fashioned out of eagle-feathers, but the heat of the sun melted the wax that held them together. And here I am,

I thought, privileged to do what kings and princes were unable to do in ages past. Such were the musings that occupied my thoughts. And that was what turned the trip into the enjoyable experience that it was. Had I directed my thoughts to plane crashes and skyjacking—well, you can imagine how that would have worked out!

So it's your job to find out all you can about where you want to go. It's your job to bring the unknown more into the realm of the known.

It doesn't make sense to consider yourself abnormal and berate yourself because you crave the familiar and the known. With the right mind-set, however, you can learn to venture out.

Switching Bases

I (SAS) recently visited friends in Texas. Wherever I went in that city, I thought of that house, not my home in New York, as my immediate home base. Wherever you go, you can create a temporary home base. If you're traveling by bus (sightseeing on an extended trip), let that bus become your home base. If you're traveling by car, let the car become your home base. If you're staying at a hotel, that becomes your home base—and so on.

People who travel a lot become very adept at switching bases. When they go to another city, they frequently check in at the same hotel chain. It's probably no mere coincidence that chain hotel rooms look the same. Yes, there's the financial aspect; it's cheaper when management can buy in quantity. But I think another reason is that management knows people are more comfortable in familiar surroundings. You can go all over the world and check into any chain hotel and, except for some local variations and color, you get pretty much the same accommodations.

Have you ever watched a square dance? There's one part where the partners dance in a circle in opposite directions, passing from one person to another until they're back in the same place. As they let go of one person's hand, they immediately reach for another person's hand—and so on. So they are always holding someone's hand as they move along. Well, traveling is pretty much like that, too. You let go of one place—and you immediately start thinking of another. You say good-bye to your friends at one airport—you greet other friends at another airport.

The only thing is that you have to become more skill-ful, more agile at switching bases. As soon as you let go of one home base, you latch onto another. It doesn't have to be an actual, physical base. That's not important. It should be more a matter of mind. When people go somewhere, they usually happily anticipate being in the new place (seeing new surroundings, meeting people). They're already starting to think of the place they're going to as their new base of operations.

Free as a Bird

Dr. Desmond Morris suggests that the fear of being alone in a wide open space may have been programmed in the human brain as a protective mechanism. This goes back in our ancestry, many thousands of years ago, when we lived as members of a hunting tribe. Being alone in a field, or anywhere away from the tribe, would have meant certain danger. Thus, fear of leaving the tribe (with its relative safety) had survival value, and this trait was passed on to the next generation. So perhaps even today this ancient inborn fear is still with us.

Yet I (SSJ) always thought the expression, "free as a bird," was an apt one; after all, can't a bird fly wherever it wants to—without restriction? But I discovered that's not so, that birds are also confined to certain boundaries just as animals and people are.

I recently read a story about birds (*Reader's Digest*: "Birds Live in Nature's Invisible Cage" by John and Jean George) that may be astonishing to the non-bird-watcher. Bird behavior, the authors tell us, "is so rigidly fixed that birds are . . . slaves to the air they fly through." One of the examples they gave was that of a cardinal whose home base had just been stripped of trees by bulldozers to make way for a new development. "As we watched," they wrote, "the bird flew about 400 feet, then suddenly back-winged as if he had hit an invisible wall. After flapping to earth, he flew off in another direction, only to smash into another invisible barrier." The boundaries of its territory were so firmly fixed in its mind that it was literally unable to fly across the clearing to safety. There were predator screech owls in the adjacent woods, and, just as they predicted, the authors found their cardinal's bloodstained feathers the following morning.

Territorial instincts are strongest in birds. Their forebrains are not well-developed, so they rely more on instincts in order to survive. (The territorial instinct helps to establish and maintain pair information, thus aiding the survival of the species.) Of course, we humans also operate by instinct in many ways. But in our species, the role of instinct is attenuated; it doesn't play such an important role in regulating behavior. We can rely on our large thinking brain. We can reason, we can question, and we can make creative use of imagery. As human beings, we have the capacity to see a situation in a new light. We also have the ability to *redefine* a situation and read new meanings into a situation.

So, make the most of your thinking cortex! Instead of narrowly outlining a certain territory and saying, "this is *my* specific area (*my* block, *my* neighborhood, *my* house, etc.)," you can mentally enlarge that same territory to encompass a much wider space. "This whole city or this whole country or this whole world is 'mine.' I'm still in 'my' safe place; I belong here."

The unfortunate bird was unable to redefine its area. He couldn't see the overall situation and judge it from a different perspective. All he could do was obey and give in to the instinct he was programmed for.

But *you're* in a position to do otherwise!

CHAPTER 15

Gaining Confidence by Doing

"No one can make you feel inferior
without your consent."
—*Eleanor Roosevelt*

A Life of Their Own

THE CURIOUS THING about panic attacks is that they soon
begin to take on a life of their own. You think about
them as you go about your daily activities; you worry
about them; you read avidly about them; you talk to
doctors about them. After a while, the panic attacks
become an important part of your life. The minute you
open your eyes in the morning, "It" is there—with a
capital I!

That's why we're always telling our clients how important it is to get interested—*really* interested—in something other than panic attacks. Something that brings you
in contact with other people. Perhaps a little business of
your own, a club, a Bible study group, or volunteer
work. You know, of course, that the mind can only think
of one thing at a time; if you have a growing interest in
whatever it may be, that interest, by its very presence in
your life, will push away the constant grim reminder of
panic attacks. But if you lie around the house staring into
space (asking over and over again, "Why me?"), or
watching one foolish TV show after another, how can
you expect your life to change??

All any therapy can do is help you to help yourself.
Even if you go to a therapist, all he can do is point you in

the right direction so that your body/mind can heal itself. The therapist can't think for you. He only helps you gain new insights that enable you to tackle your problems in a different way. Sure, this book can help; other books can help. But you have to sift through all this (and other) information, and put to work those suggestions that seem reasonable and right to you. If one thing doesn't work, try another. It's your willingness to apply this information that will ultimately change things and make the situation better.

So the bottom line is this: *You* have to want to get well; *you* have to do the things that will get you well. Nobody else can do them for you.

Developing a Real Interest

A number of phobia organizations and clinics are teaching the following method as a means of controlling panic. When a panic attack comes on or when you become anxious (so this system teaches), you're supposed to immediately measure the level of anxiety you're at—and you rate it on a scale from one to ten. (One is the lowest, ten the highest.) Then, you're supposed to watch your level of anxiety go up or down. ("I'm at a five now; now it's going up to an eight; now it's going down to a six," and so on.) It is hoped that playing this numbers game will somehow disrupt the rising barometer of panic and make it come down again.

This method not only strikes us as a bit too contrived, but, most important, we really question its effectiveness. (Maybe it does work for some, but, of course, we've been seeing people for whom this method hasn't worked.) The main reason we disapprove of this method is because it rivets attention on the Self; on the moment of panic; on the physical symptoms. And, as we pointed out, one of the things that causes the panic attacks to come in the first place is this habit of introspection, of focusing too much on the Self. Sufferers of panic attacks, as we mentioned earlier, have tendencies to question all the time,

How am I feeling? What does this symptom mean? It's this caring so much how one is feeling every single minute—and the unwillingness to tolerate any uncomfortable moments—that are at the heart of this problem.

In addition to the counting and rating oneself on a scale from one to ten, you're also supposed to, according to the method, concentrate on the here and now—by looking at trees, watching cars pass, for example. But again, we think this method is counterproductive *if* it's done in a frenzied attempt to stave off the panic attack. If the person's self-talk is something like this: "Quick—I must distract myself—look at the tree, look at the tree, concentrate on the tree!" This is not to say that one cannot use this method in a much better way. I've done this many times myself. The better way would be to really stop and *look* at the trees . . . the flowers . . . to take delight in their beauty!

Sometimes, when I have several important errands to do and I catch myself walking too fast, rushing around, I deliberately slow down, stop, and really look at my surroundings with the intent to enjoy. I might stop to admire the delicate colors of a rose in somebody's garden. Or look up at the sunset and enjoy the riot of colors I see and try to imagine how I would paint it. This pause for beauty refreshes me and it gives me a new perspective on life. (I think: "This errand I'm rushing to do—is it really so important from a cosmic view? Will anyone care a year from now? Will I? So what if I don't get it all done today . . . there's always tomorrow. Let me enjoy today, let me see the beauty now, while I can.")

But you cannot refresh your nervous system if you're frantically searching for something, anything, in a grasping way—in an attempt to divert your attention. On the contrary, it will tend to do the opposite—it will make you more nervous. Why? Because you just know normal people don't go around saying, in desperation, "Look at the tree, look at the tree." So, part of your mind (that stern Self that's always looking at you with such a critical eye) starts to mumble, "Tsk . . . tsk . . . tsk. . . . There's something not-quite-right here!" And this thought scares you all over again.

When you're walking down the street, half thinking of a panic attack, it's a little bit late to be acquiring a burning interest in something else. This has to be done way before. You have to prepare your mind. Ideas just don't grow out of the air. You have to have some input—and then, out of that, you gradually develop new interests. Something strikes your fancy; something touches off a new concept. Then you just follow your own bent and guide these budding ideas into new channels. Here are a few examples from my (SAS) own experiences.

Some years ago, I worked at a hospital. There I met a group of French-speaking employees with whom I became quite friendly. We often had lunch together. That prompted me to renew my study of high school French. Every day, I would write down vocabulary on index cards and I would memorize them as I walked or waited for the train or the elevator. (Index cards are easy to carry in your hand or your pocket.) My goal was to memorize thirty words a day. I'd forget twenty—but even so, I made progress. My pleasure at my increased fluency in the language prompted me to study with even greater zeal. And that's how interests grow: through pleasurable feedback.

At another time in my life, I used to write poetry. Constantly. I'd carry a little notebook with me—and I'd be scribbling away on the train, every day on my way to work. It kept me so occupied. I'd often look up in astonishment: "What? Is this my station—already?"

While I (SSJ) was attending medical school, I took a part-time job. I purposely took a job that was so boring and uninspiring that my mind would be freed to study and think. I also used the method of writing out my lessons and study material on index cards, and I'd memorize this information during the day, as I went along doing repetitive tasks.

You, too, can choose an area of study—something you always wanted to do but never found the time before. Well, now is the time. Not only will you become an "expert" on your favorite topic, but you'll also be so busy you won't have time to worry about panic attacks.

So doesn't it make more sense to develop a real interest in something—and use that as a focal point—rather than counting the cracks in the sidewalk?

Do You See How Far You Can Go?

Some phobia organizations teach the following: See how far you can go without panicking—and then, if you panic, turn back, go home, and try again another day.

But that's exactly what you've been doing! And, as you've discovered, that doesn't work at all. And why should it? Even if you're feeling all right at the moment, can you predict how you'll feel twenty minutes from now? So, if you go too far and "it" happens (this mindset tells you), how will you get back in time to your safe place? This viewpoint discourages you from ever going too far from home.

The Moment of Truth

Suppose you start to do something or go somewhere and you're suddenly hit with the realization: "I can't back out now!" What do you do when you arrive at that point of no return? How do you handle it?

You have to know that this is the moment you start doing all those things to relax you: To start breathing slowly. To start to drop those muscles to the floor and let gravity pull at them. To do the QR or the First Aid. There may be a powerful physical need to hyperventilate. (After all, you've already aroused your sentry by that thought: "Well, this is it . . . there's no turning back now . . . I must go through with it, come hell or high water!")

So that's pretty scary. That's when that timid, dependent child in you cries, "Ooh, I can't stand it!!" But just speak firmly to that child. Not harshly, but firmly. Say things like: "C'mon, honey, that's OK." Or: "C'mon, let's show 'em the stuff you're made of . . ." As each moment passes—and you find you haven't disintegrated yet—remind yourself of this fact. Keep on reminding yourself. Tell yourself how fine you're doing, under the circumstances. (Talk nicely: Remember, you're talking to a small, frightened child.) Never mind that you're quaking in your boots; that's not the point. The point is you are already in a situation, you're finally doing it (whatever "it" is for you). You've taken action. So congratulate yourself for this. Be proud. This is cause for celebration, not censure. The nervousness—don't worry about it. It'll subside later on, after you get more experienced in whatever it is you're doing.

I remember when I was learning to drive—and the first time I drove on the highway. Was I scared? You bet! I was with my husband—and as I slid over to take the wheel, I reviewed in my mind all my strong points: I'd done very well driving in the streets. I'd already gone up and down hills—even steep hills. I'm a careful, sane driver. My husband had confidence in my driving ability. (If he could turn over his precious car to me, I must really be doing great!) I simply ignored the feelings of fear because I know those feelings aren't particularly significant. Anybody doing something like this for the first time would be nervous. (Sure, I know there are hotshot boys who wouldn't be afraid to drive on the highway—but they're not me.)

So, instead of berating myself for not being cool—or wishing I wasn't there—I concentrated on what I was doing and on relaxing myself. (I did the slow abdominal breathing; I made my body heavy, and so on.) And as I drove along, I began to enjoy the scenery, which was so beautiful (we were in the Catskill Mountain region). Afterward, when it was over, I felt as exhilarated as if I'd just won a prize! Sentences like this were dancing in my head: "Wow, I did it—I really did it!" "I'm a driver now." "It was a lot easier than I thought!" "I'm brave, I can do it, I've got what it takes," and so on.

This is how confidence is built—slowly, bit by bit. Confidence doesn't come from reading a book on it or by programming yourself, "I will have confidence." (Positive thinking can be a great help, but it doesn't amount to a hill of beans, as far as developing confidence, if there's no accompanying action.) Confidence comes from the positive thoughts generated by the *doing*.

So you don't wait for confidence to come knocking at your door in order for you to start doing. That's putting it all backward. Confidence just naturally builds up from all those afterthoughts (i.e., your thoughts after the event) that say, "Hooray, I *did* it!"

That Safe Person

You really don't need a safe person. You *are* that safe person. Think of it: Everything you need you already have. It's all inside of you. We are, each of us, whole and sufficient for what we have to do. The hope, the courage, the life force, if you will—is inside us. And we can call on this source of strength and bring it out whenever we want to!

Even what we call outside sources of strength are still inside of us—in our own minds. The books you've read, the people you know, the people you love, the God you believe in—aren't all these things an intricate part of your Self?

An old legend tells that when Man was first made, all the angels were jealous because Man was given courage derived from the Divine Spark itself. So the angels conspired to hide this knowledge from Man, and they looked around for a hiding place. One angel said, "Let's hide it in the sky." Another said, "Let's put it into the earth." Still another said, "Let's throw it into the water." But one wise angel said, "No, let's hide it in the heart of Man himself. He'll never think of looking there!"

You're OK!

Sometimes it's hard to convince a person that he's normal, that his nervous system is functioning just fine. Despite rational explanations, some people—for some reason, want to hold on to the belief that they're sick. Many psychologists slyly suggest there is a manipulative factor at work here. Yet Dr. Weekes writes: "I have rarely met the agoraphobic man or woman who has no wish to recover."

We're just not sure who's right—or maybe there is some validity in both points of view. At any rate, with some people there's a recurrent, underlying phrase that runs like a leitmotif throughout their thoughts: "Something is wrong with me"—despite evidence to the contrary.

For example, I once had a client who could only function very well within a certain boundary—a ten-block perimeter from his house. As soon as he left his area, he would promptly get a panic attack. One day, about two weeks after he joined the program, a friend of his passed away, and he felt he had to visit the family to pay his respects. The only trouble was that the house was some distance away, out of his "boundary." But he drove there anyhow.

On the way home, even before he got into his car, he was overwhelmed by panic. He described to me his "wild ride" home—passing buses and cars and scooting in and out of traffic. It was only when his car finally screeched to a halt in front of his house that he could let go and relax. He therefore knew there was something inherently wrong with his nervous system.

"Look," I pointed out to him, "you were driving in heavy rush-hour traffic. On the way home, you must have passed hundreds and hundreds, if not thousands, of cars. Throughout all that crazy New York traffic, you were maneuvering your car successfully. Your nervous system was able to respond accurately to the thousands of clues bombarding your senses. With all that you arrived home safely. And you want to tell me something is wrong with your nervous system?"

I never found out what subsequently became of this client. He quit the program the following week.

The Urge to Run Away

When you experience a panic attack (or when you feel one is imminent), you get a strong, unmistakable urge to run away. It has little to do with any voluntary desire; it's an automatic response that occurs whenever the sentry is aroused. In fact, whenever you get the urge to run away, that's a pretty sure sign that your fight-or-flight instinct is activated. (That's what the phrase describes, doesn't it?)

But please note: The urge to run away when the hypothalamus is aroused is *not* abnormal. That's how the body was designed: During a time of danger, nature wants to help you get out of the way.

But if you *know* there's no danger, if you know it's just your own nervous over-reaction, do *not* give in to the urge to run away. What do you do? You immediately go into the QR. Or the First Aid Treatment. Once the sentry quiets down the urge to run disappears.

If you give in to the urge to run, it only makes you feel (later) defeated and angry at yourself. Whereas if you don't run away but calm yourself instead, you feel (later) a triumphant sense of victory. (Which would you rather have—the short-term or the long-term gain?)

Remember, as you continue to follow this program, the sympathetic nervous system will calm down. And as it calms down, your habitual over-reaction diminishes.

Here's a letter from one of our clients. He writes:

> I'm feeling stronger from the improved diet and exercise in following the program, so I decided to take an evening walk to a nearby movie theater and see a film. I packed some cottage cheese, whole wheat crackers, raisins, and a nectarine and set off into the night, aware of the "anticipatory anxiety" about going to a long movie alone, but determined to relax through any "episdoes" that might arrive during the night. There were several mild rev-ups, but instead of bolting out of the theater, I kept reminding

myself of everything I learned from the PASS program and from Dr. Weekes's book, and repeated the QR and kept catching myself tensing my muscles and coaching myself to relax them—to "let go"—and telling myself I was physically OK: that the worst that could happen would be I would scare myself into being very uncomfortable and also that I could choose *not* to do so.

After a while and after eating, things cleared up and my walk back home late at night (which I had also been concerned about earlier) was absolutely jubilant because of doing the right things and practicing the right attitude. I know it may sound simple and corny, but it was really quite a *triumph*! I learned how wonderful and enjoyable something can become if you don't view it as a dreadful task, and if you keep reminding yourself that you're really healthy.

By the way, this letter was written about a year ago. Recently, this young man called me just to say hello. He's doing fine, he said. He now goes on trains, planes, everything—"without batting an eyelash."

Feeling Trapped

One of the characteristics of agoraphobia is that the person is constantly seeing himself, in almost any situation he finds himself, as the victim, the "trapped," to coin a word.

Take, for example, the woman who is afraid of crossing a bridge, especially in heavy traffic. If you ask her why she's afraid, she explains she's afraid of "being trapped there," of not being able to escape when those feelings come over her.

In order to conquer this fear, certain changes have to be made to diminish the (physical) overreaction to the situation, and to alter her *perception* of the situation. In other words, body and mind.

The Body: To make sure she's not letting herself get run-down again. To eat well, practice relaxation, do daily exercise. To bring food along for the trip, remembering that stress uses up a lot of energy. This is all preliminary preparation, the background work. Just commonsense precautions (all these things tend to lower the blood lactate level, stabilize the blood sugar, calm the nervous system).

The Mind: To learn more about bridges (how they are constructed, the history of your bridge, etc.) This information might seem to be irrelevant, but it's really not. Whatever becomes more familiar, more comprehensible, also becomes less threatening.

It's also essential that she begin to see the situation from a different perspective. After all, she's not on the bridge simply by chance. She's either going somewhere or she's coming home. The bridge is there for a reason, too; there's an obstacle—a river, a highway—and the bridge was built in order to make it easier (or possible) for people to cross to the other side. So she's using the bridge in order to get where she's going; the bridge isn't using her! In other words, she's not a helpless victim who happens to be caught on a bridge. She's there for a reason.

If you keep seeing the fear only as an outside force that you have nothing to do with, then you're only delaying your own recovery. Even if you're taking medication, you still have to be responsible for the way you eat, think, manage stress, etc. A pill can't cure you. It's just another one of those paradoxes: Once you see this problem as something you yourself have a lot to do with, you'll have a much better handle on it.

I (SAS) remember reading a story in the newspaper a few years ago about a group of mountain climbers who were trapped in a cave when a landslide occurred. They were all eventually rescued. But it's interesting to note that the leader warned the group to lie quietly in order to conserve oxygen because relaxed muscles don't need as much oxygen.

But what do *you* do when you feel trapped? You immediately tense all your muscles (using up oxygen and making more lactic acid) as you frantically look for an exit. If you keep on saying to yourself, "I'm trapped," it's like waving a red flag in front of a bull. Because "I'm trapped" means to prepare the body to flee. Words are important. They're the symbols that pave the way for our thoughts to follow.

So use calming, comforting words. Change your viewpoint. Throw away that victim mentality; see yourself as brave. See yourself as a *user* of modern technology (bridges, cars, trains, etc.). These inventions provide important services, and they enable us to get where we want to go.

The Escape Hatch

I remember once reading about an ancient battle involving an invasion. The invading army arrived in ships, and after they landed, the commander ordered all the ships to be burned.

Many people go into a situation with the mind-set to retreat—even before they get there. They are armed with knowledge, but they don't really intend to use it; their thoughts are already focused on the escape hatch. (Dr. Weekes says that people will go 99 percent of the way but are unwilling to go that extra 1 percent that will bring them victory.)

But you can't have this attitude and expect at the same time to be calm and serene. Why? Because that mind-set brings still more tension to the situation. Instead of quieting you, it presents you with yet another tension-provoking option and more questions: How will I get out of it? What will I say? How will I explain this to my friends? What'll they think of me? Will they know my secret? And how can I explain this to myself? Am I really a coward at heart?

So this is really the key: Go into a situation fully armed and prepared, but without the mental reservation, "Well, if I start getting a little nervous, I'll just make up an excuse and leave." It's difficult under such conditions to practice the QR. It's difficult to be tranquil when a good part of your mind is already on the exit door.

It's far better—and really easier (although you may not believe it now)—to just burn all your bridges behind you!

Going Through Setback

This phrase seems to be in common usage, but I often wonder if it isn't unnecessarily alarming. A setback implies setting yourself back—in other words, cancelling out any gains made. And who wants to do that?

But think of it this way: Whatever progress is made is seldom, if ever, a complete success from start to finish. If you were to chart success on a graph, it would never be a straight up, up, up line. Rather, it would be like the stock market graphs you see in the newspapers—a series of wiggly lines going up and down, with plateaus in between. Yet, over the long haul (if you picked the right stock, that is), there would be a definite rise.

In nature, too, there are cyclical changes: the tides, day and night, the seasons, the weather. There is always ebb and flow, whether we're talking about electromagnetic waves or waves in the ocean. Everywhere you look you see this cyclical occurrence in nature. If this is true of nature, why shouldn't it be true of us? Aren't we part of nature?

So please don't be unduly alarmed if tomorrow you are not feeling as energetic as yesterday. Or if tomorrow it's a bit harder to do something that was easier last week. (This may be due to hormonal change—again, the cycle.) Consider this normal, and not deserving of the title, "setback." Just accept this, and wait patiently for that upward swing again.

One more thing about setback. During and following a cold or the flu, you feel depressed. Depression is just part of the syndrome that goes with a cold or the flu—like aches and pains or fever. So it's nothing to worry about; it'll pass. The feeling of not wanting to do very much at this time (except just lying in bed passively) is nature's way of helping your body to rest and recover.

Any Roadblocks?

If, after following the program for a while, you still find it difficult to go out, our advice is to look for a road block. A road block is something that's obstructing your progress, something that gets in the way. Usually it's something minor, something that can easily be remedied.

What is it in your case? And how can you go about removing it? Think about it.

Ask yourself these questions:

Are my panic attacks helping me gain something I think I might otherwise not have (like people paying more attention to me)?

Do the panic attacks give me a legitimate excuse, a way out, to avoid doing something I really don't want to do?

Do I use the panic attacks as an excuse for not living up to my perfectionist standard? "Sure, if I didn't have the panic attacks, I could be (or do) such-and-such." Am I reluctant to give up this excuse because I *may* find out I'm really not so perfect or gifted after all?

If the answers to the above questions are yes, you can help yourself by thinking up *different ways* to meet those needs. After all, the underlying wishes of wanting a feeling of closeness with others, wanting to avoid overwhelming, problematic situations, wanting to be better, to improve— these are understandable human desires and nothing to be ashamed of. But one needn't use "sickness" as a means of meeting your needs. There are better and health-ier ways to satisfy those desires.

Is It Every Really Cured?

We have seen how panic attacks can start, how they can result from a combination of negative attitude, too much stress, poor health habits, a high sugar diet. We know there is a genetic predisposition. So you correct these lifestyle situations and the panic attacks go away.

But are you really cured? you ask. Or are the panic

attacks merely arrested? Doesn't the genetic factor mean they could come back?

Yes, they could *if* you neglect your health again. *If* you go back to your old ways: too much stress, the wrong foods, pushing yourself beyond endurance. Yet even if this happens, even if the panic attacks do come back, you know what to do. It's no mystery anymore.

Remember this: The knowledge and strength you gained from this experience can never be lost. What you did before, you can do again!

But what does it really mean to be cured? Does it mean never, ever being afraid? No. (As one person once put down on his PASS-Group application, "My goal is never, ever to feel fear again.") As long as there is life, there will be fear, doubt, insecurity. It's just the way life is.

So if you *are* sometimes fearful, sometimes insecure and worried—well, what of it? Welcome to the human race!

PART IV

Twenty Personal Stories—Told by the People Who Lived Them

Alice's Story

I was born in Brooklyn. I grew up there and went to school there. Then, a few years after I got married, I moved to Vermont. That was about twenty years ago—and then the panic attacks began. I couldn't leave my home without suffering a severe panic attack. This prevented me from doing many things. I couldn't shop where I wanted; I couldn't even go to church. And I was extremely limited in the distance I could travel. At one point, I couldn't even go to the mailbox! My one wish was to be well enough to be able to come back to Brooklyn to visit my family.

Before the panic attacks began, I was the type of person who was always on the go. The attacks came in stages—first, I didn't want to go out alone; then, I couldn't go out at all, and finally, I became very uncomfortable even when I was alone in the house. My husband would tell people I was sick. It's very embarrassing to explain what's really wrong.

I was in private therapy for six years, without success. Then, finally, I couldn't see the point of sitting in a doctor's office week after week and just talking. I called the mental health clinic where I live, and they sent someone to my house to take me out a little. We would go out walking as far as I could go, and then we'd come back. I felt this was making progress, compared to the therapy.

But a few months later, while leafing through a *TV Guide,* I saw an ad for PASS and decided to give it a try. I started the program, and, on August 16, 1983, just four months after I joined PASS, my wish to come to Brooklyn finally came true!

The trip coming down from Vermont was great. There were six of us in the car: my daughter, her husband (who was driving), their three children, and me. I found myself enjoying everything—the scenery, the ride. It was a long trip, so we stopped to eat several times along the thruway. I remember what my counselor said and didn't try to see the whole journey all at once, but broke it all down into small "baby" steps. Naturally, I was excited (who wouldn't be?), but I didn't think of it as nervousness—just a pleasant excitement and wonderful anticipation. After all, my dream of a lifetime was coming true!

Can you imagine how I felt when I finally saw the New York skyline? (The last time I saw it was in 1962!) After driving through Brooklyn, we went to Staten Island, where my brother now lives. Going over the Verrazano Bridge was especially thrilling for me because I used to live near the park that later became the base of the bridge. What a change in the old neighborhood! And what a reception I got at my brother's house! There was a huge banner on display that said, "Welcome Home Aunt Alice." But until they actually saw me stepping out of the car, my relatives couldn't believe I really made that trip!

That winter, back in Vermont, we were snowed in much of the time. But I had so many warm memories to remember about my trip to New York. I've since been on many other trips (including Brooklyn again), but this trip will always stand out as one of the highlights of my life.

I never think of my "phobia" anymore. I just think of good things when I go someplace. You have to try new things. If you don't, you miss out on a lot. And you never know you CAN, if you don't try.

What I learned is that I can do it. Life doesn't scare me anymore.

Bob's Story

I'm eighteen years old, and I live on a farm. I joined PASS three months ago because I had this terrified fear of leaving home. I wanted to learn to cope with problems and to find peace within myself.

The way my panic attacks started was this: I was with my cousin, and we went to a nearby town. We stopped over in a store, but on the way back—I don't know, out of nowhere (that's what really scared me!), I got this enormous panic attack. But I couldn't go right back home. My cousin was driving and he had to make several stops. I felt real shaky and I was afraid of everything, because I had never experienced anything like this before. I couldn't understand what was happening to me. I thought I was going nuts—or dying or something!

That's when I started falling out of society; that was the beginning. Little by little, I began staying home. The more time went by, the more I'd stay home. I didn't really drop out of school at this point. I would *try* to go—but then I'd get panicky and have to run home. I didn't ask anybody; I'd just get in the car and leave. The principal knew I was having problems, and he was very good about it. I had started to see a psychologist at that time, and she helped me out by talking to the principal about me. But the more I would try to stay and fight—because I didn't know how to do it the *right* way—the worse it got.

That summer, to me, was a living hell. I didn't find out about PASS until December—and my panic attacks began in November, the year before. The second panic attack was when my buddy and I were drinking. After that episode, I never touched alcohol again. But things weren't so bad at the beginning—they just got progressively worse. Little by little, things started to go downhill. My car burned up, so I had no trasnportation other than my parents' car. My dad was very good about it—he let me use his car. But it just seemed that one thing after another went wrong. Things went down and down until I hit an all-time low. And then, little by little, I'd make a comeback. But I didn't have the information at that time that PASS later made available to me, and I didn't have the understanding to really get me back on my feet. I remember thinking that I didn't expect to live out the summer because I thought I was dying or going crazy, and I even thought of committing suicide!

And now that I *know* what I know, I can really look back and laugh at this! But you can't tell that to somebody who's just going through the first stages of this, because they're really scared. But I would say to them, once you get a better understanding of this, it just seems there's a whole new world opening up!

Do you know what I was eating before? A lot of sugar foods, a lot of candy bars, things like potato chips that were loaded with salt, french fries, things like that. I remember telling my counselor at the beginning of the program, that I was on a very good diet! I *thought* I was, because I was also eating a lot of meat and potatoes. We've always raised our own beef on the farm, so I was brought up on a meat-and-potatoes diet. But now I'm eating five or six mini-meals and I watch what I eat. I really put together a very good diet now—and I exercise a lot. I'm in fantastic shape right now—I've never been in this good shape before!

Looking back, I see that I've made really great progress. For example, last week, my mother and I got in the car and we went to this small town, about forty miles from here, to visit my mother's friend. And then, from there, we went to another town, about ten miles away. And then we went to the Capital City Mall. But that wasn't all: We went to *another* town, which is about twenty or thirty miles from here, and we shopped around. There are two malls there. Then, we went to a government surplus store, and had lunch at a very nice restaurant. On the way back, we stopped at a garage. There was a guy there who helped me get my car, and he was surprised to see me. And then we stopped at my buddy's trailer—and he also was surprised to see me.

And you know what my method is now? I just sit there and relax and let go—and I just think good thoughts and stuff. Like: How happy I am and how good life is—things like that. I look at the good.

What advice would I give to someone just starting this program? I would say, "Don't ever give up!" Because there were times when I thought seriously of committing suicide, things looked so bleak. I remember, at one point, I even planned on staying home the rest my life . . . ! But I knew I could never do that. So don't you ever give up, either!

Brenda's Story

The panic attacks started about a month before I graduated from high school. I had just broken up with my boyfriend, so I was under great stress. I neglected my health, I didn't eat. Just knowing I was leaving high school, a secure place, and going out into the world—that, more or less combined with my personal problem—was what started the panic attacks.

I was in a very bad state. I was always having feelings of unreality. I was constantly living with this. I always used to think: Am I going to have a panic attack today? I hated to go too far from the house. I was worried I was going crazy. I was always thinking, always looking inward. Constantly. But the feelings of unreality worried me the most.

I think the basis for this worry is that people don't understand what's happening to them. So, in the back of their minds, they think something horrible is about to happen to them. Even when the doctor told me I was in excellent health, it didn't help at all. Nobody explained it to me before. I used to wonder: "What's the matter with me? Why am I like this?" So the worry continued. I remember once telling my doctor, "I don't feel like I'm really here." And he said, "Well, if you're not here, Brenda, where are you?" I didn't know at the time it's the body's way of working with stress. That's all it is. I also feel that when you're on a poor diet that it has a lot to do with it. There's a biochemical disturbance that makes these feelings of unreality. And then, when you couple this with "inwardness," it only makes it worse, naturally. And then you really have a problem!

After I left high school, I got a job. I worked for this one company for two and a half years. Then my boyfriend and I (the one I had broken up with before) got together again. I had known him for a long time—we were childhood sweethearts—and he was pleading with me to go back with him. So I did—and we got married.

Six months later, I quit my job because I had to get up very early and hassle with buses, and so on—and it was just too much for me to handle. I had been taking buses in to work after I started getting panic attacks in the subway. The panic attacks were constantly on my mind. I wasn't able to go into a restaurant. I would get panic attacks just waiting for food to come. Then it went from restaurants to stores. I was getting panic attacks in stores, so I couldn't go into a store. The panic attacks soon stopped me from going to other places, too, like movies. It really restricted me because it spilled over into so many places.

I was in therapy before I joined this program. I had gone to a psychologist for over a year, and I wasn't getting anywhere. What he did for me was put me under hypnosis for about twenty minutes. That was very good. That was the only thing that was helpful—the relaxation. But here, with this program, I developed my own way of relaxing, my own technique. But, basically, at that point (when I was with the psychologist) I wasn't cured and I seemed to be getting nowhere. It was only after I joined this program that things really fell into place, with the change of diet, with the change in my attitude, with the relaxation, exercise, and so on. It was everything *combined—that* was the most important thing, that's what helped me.

At first, it was difficult to incorporate all these things into my lifestyle. But I was determined because I couldn't live like that anymore. I couldn't handle the constant fear on my shoulders. But getting back to the program—I knew I had to do things. I knew that the more I practiced, the more I'd get out of it. I hated to get in the car and go for an hour's drive. I started carrying the PASS book with me, carrying the tape with me (that was my little "security" then). This was after I'd been on the program—I'd say, about two months. I had a very poor diet before. I was eating a lot of things I wasn't supposed to, and I was eating a lot of sugar. No green vegetables, not enough protein—none of the things I was supposed to be eating.

It was a very gradual, not a sudden, improvement. I really think it was the combined approach that helped me. I can see now how everything works together—the seven steps. Because you apply each thing differently. Just having the knowledge of how your body/mind works— the nervous system and so on—gives you a better understanding of what's happening to you. Knowing what I'm supposed to eat—*that* makes a little less stress. Taking certain vitamins—*that* takes a chunk out of the stress. So—everything *combined* really diminishes anxiety.

My life is so different now from what it was! I look back in amazement! Being able to leave the house and not ever worrying about "what-if"; getting rid of that constant tension I had; just to leave the house and go to a store—it's wonderful! I think back—before, I used to make up so many excuses for not going out. And when I did go out, I could only go up to a certain point. And I also couldn't leave the house before 10:30 or 11 o'clock in the morning. Now, I can leave the house 8, 9—it doesn't matter. I don't have that time limit. And I go anywhere. I drive anywhere.

Before, I was so limited—I couldn't do many things. Now, I'm in and out of restaurants (only those with salad bars!). I take public transportation; I go shopping. In fact, I *love* to go shopping now. I usually go by myself or with my girlfriends. I drive my friends around from store to store, which gives me a *great* feeling. I always take food along when I'm driving. I might have a peach, yogurt, cantaloupe slices in a little container, cheese, whole wheat crackers, a container of soup. (Sometimes I think I could go on a two-week safari!) I just nibble along the way, as I go. By the way, I must say—not only didn't I gain weight using this method of frequent eating, but I lost six pounds!

Right now, my son is going to be in a play. He has rehearsals three times a week, so I take him and pick him up. I could let my husband do this, but, as I said, this gives me a great feeling, so I do it. I'm really enjoying this year's hustle and bustle, but I make the time to eat right, exercise, and—believe it or not—I relax in between.

I have a better way of coping with things now, a different way of looking at them. For example, last night I didn't get much sleep—only four hours. I had a slight headache (I know the reason) and my stomach was a little queasy. But even though it was queasy, I still had my egg on whole wheat toast and a cup of tea. Before the program, I would have had just toast and tea. But now I know what my body needs. I might have felt lightheaded before and not known what caused it. But now I realize it had a lot to with my diet and my not eating whenever my stomach used to be a little upset. Because now I feel fine—no problem.

Here's another example: The other week, I went driving and I got lost. But I didn't panic, as I would have done before. I really didn't. In fact, I felt good and secure. I just told myself, "I can do it, I can find my way back." I didn't have anxiety about it. The thought now of panicking is very dim in my mind. I may *think* of it sometimes, but it's not at all like it used to be.

My husband was very supportive through all this. Sometimes we laughed together, sometimes we cried together. But this whole ordeal has brought us closer. Recently, I became a counselor for PASS. I enjoy helping people—and giving back to others what I was given.

Don's Story

The first time I had a full-fledged panic attack—I'll never forget it—was one night after I left work. I was walking down the street and it felt like somebody had hit me over the head, it was that sudden. My heart started pounding, my legs turned to jelly, I couldn't breathe—the whole bit. This got me into an anxiety state for weeks. Finally, after a couple of weeks of this constant anxiety, I confided in a friend of mine, who happens to be a therapist. And she referred me to a psychiatrist. So I went into therapy and that lasted two years.

Although I got a lot out of the therapy itself—for instance, I learned a lot about myself; it forced me to look at and resolve a lot of the conflicts in my life—it didn't help me as far as the panic attacks were concerned. It didn't give me the practical knowledge I needed in order to deal with the panic attacks. My most feared experience was driving through the tunnel and getting stuck in traffic there. One day this happened—and I thought I was going to stop breathing. It was nighttime, it was dark, and I felt just like getting out and running. It was total *panic*!

So it wasn't until I got involved with PASS that I really felt it was going to get better. This information that my counselor gave me was basic, concrete, common sense information. I didn't have to take apart my mother, my father, and this and that, to try to find out how to resolve something. I remember being so surprised when my counselor cut me short the first time I started talking about my mother, my childhood. Because I thought that was what you were supposed to say. I was in therapy at the time, and that, basically, was the vehicle they used.

I stopped smoking over a year ago. That was one of the things I wanted to do—and I finally did it. I must say, I feel *so* much better! I'll never go back to smoking. I gained weight—I was much too thin before—and I exercise, I work out. I feel really good—and I look a lot better, too.

I learned two important things from my experience with the panic attacks: (1) Perseverance. You have to stick with it. And (2) Patience. Coming from that experience, these are two things that stayed with me, that have become part of my coping skills.

I recently went into business, but the business failed. This set me back a bit, financially. But I'm young—I'm in my thirties. And I learned a lot from this experience. I realized some of the mistakes I made. So I'm going to try again soon. Nowadays, I don't give up that easily. I know that, in time, I'll make it.

My message to someone suffering from panic attacks is this: You really can get beyond it and over it. I think the key word is "acceptance." The moment I accepted the way it was, it changed everything for me for the better. That's another paradox, isn't it? But I think it's because you're taking the pressure off yourself. As soon as you say it's OK to be this way, you're freeing yourself.

Instead of saying, "I wish I were different" or "I wish I felt differently"—instead of saying that, you say, "This is the way I'm feeling and I'm going to accept that fact." By doing that, you take a tremendous weight off your shoulders. Because you don't have to force yourself to change; the change happens naturally.

It takes time. My improvement was gradual. That's how I learned to be patient and to stick with it. You can't give up on yourself.

Elaine's Story

My story begins five years ago, in a car. I had been having a rushed day of shopping with my sister and when I turned to go home, the road looked strange. I wasn't sure where we actually were. After I made several turns in the road (I was driving), a panic attack just hit me out of the blue! After I pulled off the road, we got a police car to stop and help, and I was taken to the emergency room of a nearby hospital.

Up until then, hyperventilation wasn't even a word in my vocabulary—and I know how casually people use this term. But I experienced it to the point of total stiffness throughout my body. After a similar occurrence in a shopping mall and a return to the hospital emergency room, the doctor sent me for extensive testing for possible ear problems.

When these tests came back negative, I was told to see a psychologist. I worked with him for a couple of months. It did help some, but not enough to bring me back to the so-called "normalness" of before.

If you've never experienced this personally, it's very hard for anyone to actually relate to those feelings that came over me. Feelings of complete panic would set in with no warnings at all—or so it seemed. To venture out alone was impossible. I began to plan all my trips away from the house with my husband, because it was "safe" when I was with him. A trip to the grocery store was a grueling adventure. I would go down each aisle and hope there was no one there I knew so that I wouldn't have to stop and talk. The checkout line loomed ahead of me a mile long, and it felt like my legs didn't want to hold me up.

At church, just trying to sit in a pew and watch the usher rope off the back pews was unbearable. At one service, we had to get up and leave. The noise level of crowds tripled to my ears. Sometimes, I could hardly stand the sounds of people altogether.

But my main problem was driving a car alone. It seemed it took more patience than I could muster to stay at an intersection and wait out the panic scene in my head. I can still remember vividly sitting at the light stop, waiting for left turns and trying to make sense of everything around me (those lights seemed *days* long!). The muscles of my legs and body were so tensed up all the time that I wonder now how on earth I could even have walked by myself! And the fact that I had no idea what was really going on was frightening. I was afraid to talk to anyone about these feelings. Who could possibly understand what was going on in my head??

When my husband saw something in the paper about PASS, he showed it to me and I sent away for information. And that eventually led me on the road to recovery. Let me tell you that without the help and understanding of my counselor, Jaye, I don't know in what condition I'd be in today! On Saturdays, we had our telephone sessions, and I always looked forward to that. I was all ears and very eager to listen to every word she said. I did exactly as she told me, with full confidence. I thought if she got well, then I would, also. I learned exactly what was happening to me and I started to put the whole picture together.

The main changes in my life have been to learn to relax, to change my way of acting *completely*, and just to learn to slow down and live. The trick in learning to relax to the fullest is to *practice*. I do the relaxation tape almost daily, so now my body is tuned to relax completely at a given signal. I abstain from all forms of sugar (other than what's in fruit, etc.). This helped "stabilize" my blood sugar and enabled me to have a more steady feeling. I eat plain old, good food—fruits, vegetables, fish, chicken, yogurt, and some red meat occasionally. Whole grain breads and crackers are now staples in my diet. Since I found caffeine to be intolerable to my system, I eliminated it. After many months on this diet, my weight dropped and I feel so much stronger and better. The weight loss is an added benefit.

Frank's Story

I'm a free-lance writer and I also write music—so my life is riddled with stress and tension, as far as that's concerned. You've heard of a Type A personality? Well, I'm a Triple-A personality!

My life, before I started this program, was intolerable. I was in persistent and lengthy states of tension and anxiety. It was a living hell. As far as I'm concerned, I was one step away from needing to be locked up! I was living in fear constantly; I really considered I was having a nervous breakdown! I couldn't sleep nights. It was difficult for me to commit myself to anything—social or in business—because of my panic attacks. I used to be frightened of every new symptom—especially in my chest and head. These severe symptoms dominated me and stifled my goals in life. I was overly conscious of doing, eating, or thinking about anything that might add stress or cause one of these attacks that I was constantly on my guard against. I desperately sought ways to control these symptoms and I needed constant reassurance that I was not in any physical or medical danger. Yet I wanted very much to be able to resume living, enjoying life and pursuing my goals without being constantly on guard. One day, my girlfriend showed me an article in *Family Circle* magazine that mentioned PASS, and that's how I joined the program.

I live in New York, and my recent trip to California

was probably the highlight, the culmination of my endeavors. I know you think it was pretty daring on my part, but my "secret" was to stop viewing it as something daring! The thing is to break the habit of viewing something as being an obstacle or being something huge. For example, one day I had to take a bus to New Jersey and that was sort of the first big barrier since I'd gotten into the bad habit of sitting around at home all the time, thinking that I was "ill" and couldn't go anywhere. Anyhow, I had to go to New Jersey and I really just relaxed and had a very smooth time with that trip—it involved a long subway ride followed by a long bus ride. I brought my music along, to listen to. And once I was on the bridge going to New Jersey, I thought it was great. I realized if I could do this successfully, I knew I was capable of going to California. And from that point on, whenever I thought of going to California, the phrase that I used for myself was: "I'm in the same physical condition, the same physical health, whether I'm in New York or in Montana or on Mars!" And if I remember that and accept that and believe it, then there's no reason to even think that just by going a distance away, that anything "physical" was going to happen. Of course, the logical aspect came to me pretty quickly, but the practice of applying it—that took a little while.

Of course, I had a lot of "anticipatory anxiety" about the trip. But once I was on the plane, it was fine. I used the whole arsenal of "tools" I acquired through the program and Dr. Weekes's books; I used them whenever I grew anxious or tense. I sat next to the window and watched the takeoff. Wow! And I remember, on the way back from California, we were flying just as the sun was rising above the clouds. It was just exhilarating and so beautiful to sit there and look out of the window and watch the clouds and the sky light up and turn a beautiful shade of blue. It was just wonderful!

There was one point when the plane had to drop a little bit to get out of some clouds, and my stomach was up in my throat for a few seconds. But the first thing I did, under the circumstances, was the QR. I took a couple of deep abdominal breaths and just told myself to do all the right things in terms of physical relaxation. And I was just fine within a matter of a few seconds. So everything was very successful, in terms of dealing with the anxiety.

Another valuable thing about taking that trip to California is that I can now recall some of the more wonderful aspects of travel. Anyone with the problem of agoraphobia should look forward to tackling a little expedition, because you can use that as your visualization exercise. Like the time I went to the beach or the time I was up in a plane, looking at the clouds. Those mental "photographs"—while I enjoyed those situations—I also use them now in conjunction with my relaxation tape. When you recall or recapture something that was enjoyable to you, it not only benefits you in terms of how your immediate bodily reactions are, but it also provides that stimulus to go out and do again—and do more.

I'm still under a lot of stress—I'm always having to meet deadlines, etc.—but it doesn't get to the point of panic anymore. I just view those certain periods as times when I just have to be patient with myself. Now that I have this different approach to my work, I take periodic exercise breaks—*before* the tension builds up. I might do some stretching or some light calisthenics or dance very gently to radio music for a while (it depends on what I feel comfortable with) on any given day. Or I might do more strenuous things—like two days ago, I had all this energy, so I was out playing basketball. I kept going at it for a while, but I felt great. I'm in very good condition again, now that I've been exercising regularly. While I was in California, I played tennis with my friends, and I was as effective as ever on the tennis court. I'm really trim now, although I was never heavy, but I notice I'm in considerably better shape than the last time I was in California.

When I joined the PASS program, I was already on medication, but I was still getting panic attacks *all the time!* Now, since I started the PASS program, I decreased my dosage. In fact, during my trip to California,

I cut it down even more. And I've not had anything even *resembling* panic in quite some time. I really feel I'm dealing very effectively with the whole situation. Just by diet, exercise, attitude change, and so on, and practicing to deal with any symptoms as soon as they happen and not to react to them incorrectly. My girlfriend noticed the changes in me a lot better than anyone else because she was living with me when my condition had reached its "peak." One day, while I was in California, she was telling my other two friends—and she was beaming when she said it—"Oh, it's so great to see the change in him. He's actually able to sit in a restaurant and have a meal!" And: "He's able to just turn off the TV and come to sleep at night." Before, I had a very big problem with sleeping. The insomnia was simply unbearable.

So you see I'm a strong advocate of this entire program—because I've seen for myself what it can do!

Gloria's Story

I've had panic attacks since 1969, after an extremely emotionally stressful period I went through. The doctor put me on Valium at the time and I took the medication for five years. Then I went to another doctor, who took me off the Valium and prescribed a different kind of medication, to be taken only as needed. I never went out much then, because whenever I'd go to a crowded public place, my chest would start pounding and I'd start trembling.

I joined PASS in November of 1984 because my son was going to be married in March and I was literally walking around in a nightmare: I worried—How was I ever going to go to the wedding? What would I do when I panicked? I had been desperately looking for a program that would help me get through that day in one piece! I didn't want to be knocked out by pills. Of course, my ultimate goal was to be able to go anywhere by myself, with confidence and in control of myself, without panicking or becoming frightened.

Soon after I started the PASS program, I began to make the necessary changes in my lifestyle. I had been on a liquid diet, eating only one little meal a day, in order to lose ten pounds before the wedding. Then I stopped this diet and went on the one recommended by PASS. At the end of November, I started my program of regular exercise. I was very careful about my diet now and also about the relaxation exercises. There were a lot of people in my exercise class, and I was pleasantly surprised that I didn't feel any of the panic I used to feel in crowds.

By December, I was already feeling much better. Even my husband noticed the difference and remarked how much calmer I had become. By Christmas, I was beginning to feel a lot more optimistic about the turnaround in my life. I had some stress—some family problems at that time—but I found I really changed my outlook on things. My attitude was different now. I let things ride and I wasn't as "all strung out" as I used to be before. So the stress didn't affect me that much and I was able to cope. I also became more involved socially with the women's group of my husband's lodge.

In January, we began getting ready for the wedding in March. I talked to my counselor about being nervous at the wedding, but she somehow reassured me that all would be well. I did my relaxation session faithfully every day. We were getting a lot of phone calls now, so I used to take the phone off the hook for that half hour. In mid-January, I suddenly felt ill. I thought it might be nerves, but when I saw the doctor, he told me it was an intestinal virus. I decided not to pay attention to it, and it just cleared up by itself. I used the "worry-hour" strategy. Whenever I wanted to worry about the wedding or something else, I'd postpone the worry for a few hours and worry about it all at once. It worked for me—and I found I could relax a lot better during the day.

I had another goal before the wedding: to be able to go shopping in Bloomingdale's. So one day, I went there with my future daughter-in-law. Once in the store, I was really surprised that I didn't feel closed in, the way I used to feel. I only had a little mild fluttering in my stomach, but after a few moments it went away. I knew how to handle it.

The bridal shower was held at my house. A few days before, I called my counselor at PASS because I was getting anxious. She reassured me and told me it was perfectly normal. She advised me to do most of the cooking and baking the day before—even to clean the house before—so the day of the party all would be in order and I wouldn't have anything hanging over my head. Well, it just went beautifully. Everything was lovely. This success gave me more courage to face the wedding. And, as it turned out, I also didn't have to worry about the wedding: Everything turned out wonderful.

The weather was lovely, the bride was lovely. I wore a beige gown that really looked great on me. I also had my makeup put on by a professional—I felt like a movie star! I was so excited, but it was a happy excitement. About 300 people attended the wedding. The main event for me was when we all walked into the ballroom and they introduced us. I had a wonderful time. The evening went by so fast, I couldn't believe it. It was 2 a.m. when it was all over.

I feel this program helped me a lot. It made me realize so many things. I'm more aware now. I know what can bring on a panic attack and I see that doing the right thing helps me avoid the panic attack. I go to a lot of places by myself now. There's a big shopping mall near me and I now go there all the time. (It's really within walking distance, so I often walk there.) Before, when I had to go there, I'd hurry up with everything just to get it over with. But now I go there leisurely. I take my time, look around, and I really enjoy it. Now, whenever I go somewhere, I tend not to think "what if this, what if that." I just go straight ahead where I have to go.

Helene's Story

About a year ago, on New Year's Day, I had a panic attack, but I really didn't know what it was. I thought I was just overtired because I had been up late New Year's Eve. So it didn't upset me. (Later, I found out my intuition was right!) I didn't have another panic attack until two months later, when I went to a car show with my husband. We were walking around, and I started having these "funny feelings." I thought I was going to faint, that's how I felt. And I thought it was because I was smelling the car exhaust fumes (again, my intuition was probably correct). Anyhow, we went home; I rested a while, and I was fine. Then, in May of that year, I was in an accident where I got hit on the head. Two days later, I was with the kids in school—I'm a teacher—and they were watching a play. During the play, I had those "funny feelings" again; I thought I was going to faint. I felt really shaky, very nervous and dizzy. My first reaction was to get out of there, to get out of that room. I felt I needed fresh air. Another teacher saw me and said to me, "You better go to the doctor now and find out what's wrong with you." She knew I had the accident with my head, and she told me it might be very serious.

So I left my class with a substitute, and I went to the doctor. While driving to his office, I had the worst panic attack ever. I almost couldn't drive the car. I was so afraid I might pass out while driving and be in another accident again. And I was also nervous about going to the doctor. I wondered what he might find. So these fears were just building up inside of me, making everything worse.

But as it turned out, the x-rays were normal and the doctor found I was all right physically. A few months later, though, I had another panic attack that came out of the blue. I started having a couple of panic attacks a week, and sometimes I'd even have two or three during the day. I realized something wasn't right. So I went to the doctor again. He checked me out thoroughly and prescribed Xanax, but a very mild prescription. He tried to figure out something in my life that was causing stress and starting these attacks, but we couldn't figure out anything. He thought maybe it was something I was not consciously aware of yet.

At first, I wasn't taking the pills right, because I didn't think I needed to be taking pills; you always hear these terrible stories about people becoming addicted to them. Well, the panic attacks kept recurring, so finally I did begin to take the pills regularly. But even though I was now taking the pills the way I was supposed to, the panic attacks still crept up on me.

My mother, who knew what was going on all this time, saw an article in the paper, written by a doctor, about PASS. I kept the paper, but I still didn't call yet. I waited. Then, school was about to start again, but there was no way I could teach, the way I felt. The panic attacks kept happening more and more, and the pills were hardly working. So at that point, I called PASS and I started the program.

What I liked about this program from the start is its common-sense approach, and its one-to-one counseling. And there are steps you can take right away. Like the eating—that helped a lot. Right away, I started eating every three hours and watched what I ate. And I really noticed the difference. The exercise I started, to a certain extent, before I began the PASS program. But when I realized how important that was, I just kept it up. And the relaxation tape helped a lot. I really didn't know how tense I was until I started listening to the tape and realized afterwards, by the way I felt, how much tension I had accumulated during the day.

You know, one of my biggest problems—believe it or not—was when I had to have my hair cut. I've been going to this girl for two years, but I had a big panic attack there once, so every time I went back, it reminded me. So it wasn't easy going back. My counselor suggested that right after I listen to the relaxation tape, I should visualize being at the beauty parlor and to go through each little step in a relaxed way, in my imagination. So I did that for the four days before my appointment. It happened to be at the beginning of the PASS program, when I was really scared about getting my hair cut. Well, just before I went there, I had butterflies in my stomach. But that was the extent of it. That was it. I didn't have any "funny feelings" or anything like that. When I left the beauty parlor, I called up my counselor and yelled, "I did it! I can't believe I did it!" I was so excited and thrilled. And then, another time after that, I was in the beauty parlor to get a perm, and I was there for something like three hours. And it worked out fine, too. I really believe that visualization is a very helpful method—because it's like a dress rehearsal.

Looking back on this whole experience with panic attacks, I can see now that my biggest problem was that I was exaggerating the weird feelings I was having—whereas I should have just been ignoring them and realize that I was going to be all right. If I had known that from the beginning—instead of always worrying that something was seriously wrong with me—I would have relaxed, and it wouldn't have developed into such a big problem.

Jason's Story

My first memories of panic attacks go back to 1975; I had two or three within a couple of weeks, on the subway. A little while after that, I had an experience where I was taking a shower, and after the shower, I passed out. Fortunately, I was able to jump out of the shower when I started feeling dizzy and lightheaded. But by the time I was starting to dry myself off, I was "out." And from that point on, for some reason, every physical sensation that I had was very heightened. And I started noticing that I was getting very tense. Pretty soon after that, I had another panic attack. And at that point, I really got worried. I had been dieting very heavily and hadn't been eating—but I still didn't understand what was happening. I was actually hoping that this was something physical that I could take care of.

I went to my family doctor and he gave me a full physical checkup. He told me I was perfectly normal and that this was just "nerves." So that really started the whole process of thinking it's "mental." I said to myself:

OK, what's wrong with me? Why did I have a nervous reaction? I started to analyze everything. I thought: My life seemed normal. So it must be that I'm going crazy or cracking up inside. There must be this dark, deep thing inside that's causing me to have these terrible feelings, I thought. But I didn't share that with anyone and things got worse.

Well, I did a pretty good job of hiding it. I didn't like to admit that things were going wrong, so I let it sit with me as long as I possibly could. And that started to include whole evenings when I would just be feeling very tense; everything seemed a little weird and out of focus. Once, I went to a sporting event in mid-Manhattan, and the minute I got into the arena, I felt very disoriented. For that whole evening, I didn't know what was going on. I just knew I was very nervous and thought that something bad might happen any minute. I was with a friend, so of course I didn't say anything. I sort of sat there, gritting my teeth and counting the minutes till I could leave.

I had been seeing a therapist when this incident happened, but I didn't even tell him about some of the stuff that had been happening. I hid it from him, too, because I guess I was embarrassed. I had a lot of trouble admitting weakness. Because, at that time, I had interpreted all this as a kind of "weakness" on my part. And, at the beginning stages, I really didn't believe it was a physical thing. So I didn't share it with anyone and things got worse.

What I wound up doing was jump from doctor to doctor. For example, I went to a neurologist and had an EEG. Then I went to an ophthalmologist because the symptoms seemed to be vision-related. I had disorientation and blurred vision at times. But everything checked out OK. My parents encouraged me to go to doctors because they were convinced I'd find a cure.

Finally, my girlfriend heard about PASS on the radio and she told me to call the number. I was very hesitant. But I was kind of at my wit's end because I had exhausted the channels of dealing with it on my own.

At the time I called PASS, I wouldn't even go to a movie; I would hesitate to even drive. After a couple of telephone sessions, they gave me so much information that I never even heard of before: that what I had was common; that I wasn't "going crazy"; that there was an actual basis for this, and so on. It was the first time that anything made sense to me, really. There was a kind of cohesiveness to the whole thing. It was also great to have a male counselor and to hear that he had it, too, at one time. Because most of the information I was getting was that it was only a female-oriented kind of problem. Certainly, in light of my difficulty in admitting weakness, having a male counselor gave me a bit of momentum and impetus to improve.

Basically, my life has changed very much since I took the program, about two years ago. I don't get really worried now about doing anything. And there's nothing that I stop myself from doing if I want to do it. I also understand that I'm not going to be totally "worry-free" for the rest of my life. But I don't feel "alone." I know what this is all about and I feel that I'm now in charge of my life. I've gone back to school to get my B.S. This was something I really wanted to do, but I lacked the confidence before. I had doubts about my ability; I didn't know I could do it. But then, once this business with the panic attacks cleared up, I decided to go for it. I'm getting very good grades and I'll be getting my M.S.W. next year.

When I graduate, I'd love to hook myself up with a clinic or mental health facility that deals with phobic individuals. I want to help people—especially those who have this problem. I feel "all together" now. I have a much broader perspective of things and I'm much more confident because I've already overcome so many hurdles myself.

Marla's Story

My problem with panic attacks started when I stayed home for a couple of years with my second child when he was a baby. That's when I had a lot of time to sit and think. I felt very isolated. I didn't have too many friends then. I know that introspection is a common problem with people who have panic attacks, and that they're usually creative people. So they need other interests. I think I did have many other interests on and off before, but during those few years when I was home, I didn't. And so the jogging I started doing for exercise helped me get started again. It gave me the incentive I needed to get out of the house again and start doing things. Then, later, I got a part-time job, and that helped rebuild my confidence, too.

I had been bothered by panic attacks, actually, since I was fifteen (I'm thirty now). I was determined to find out what the heck it was. I read whatever I could find on it, but I never quite pinpointed it. I used to try to find out in my own little way if anybody else experienced this. But when I'd ask, they'd say, "Oh, I know what you mean. Everybody gets nervous once in a while." But I knew they didn't quite know what I meant. Yet, the funny part of it is that now that I *know* what it is, a few people have mentioned it to *me*.

I guess I was more fortunate than most, because the panic attacks never kept me home. With me, I never associated the panic attacks with the outdoors. Instead, the panic attacks would occur indoors—especially when I was home during those few years with my son. I started being afraid of doing things I normally used to do—like going shopping alone. Whenever I'd be in the store, I'd get that uncomfortable, panicky feeling and I'd want to leave right away.

When I first read the newspaper article about a girl who suffered from panic attacks, I couldn't believe how it described me to a T. Then, at the end of the article, it listed places where you could get help, and that's how I found PASS. What I liked about this program was that there was no medication involved. And it was done over the phone—it wasn't like you had to travel every week.

For me, the program was fairly easy to follow because I'm very disciplined about my eating habits. But I must admit that the one thing I found difficult was staying away from coffee, because I enjoy drinking coffee; I love the taste of it. So now, if I do have a little coffee now and then and find myself a little bit nervous from it or "hyper," I know why it's happening, so it doesn't bother me.

One of the best parts of the program for me was just finding out about this group and having someone explain to me exactly what I was feeling. *Why* the panic attacks were happening and what I could do about it. What's important is that you're able to slow your body down. You're more in control. Like when you feel a panic attack coming on, knowing that you can take a deep breath and do some other relaxation technique and that, just physically alone, it's going to slow you down. And knowing that when you're getting the attack, that that's the worst that can happen—that it's not going to get any worse than that. All these things are important. I started the program over a year ago now, and I haven't had any panic attacks for a long time now (knock wood!). Naturally, I feel a little bit more nervous at times, but this just tells me I have to slow down a bit—and I do. But just knowing that if I get a panic attack, I can handle it makes it so it doesn't seem to come.

Nancy's Story

Before I was on this program, I used to get three or four severe panic attacks a week. Then, after I was on the program a while, the panic attacks would only go so high; they weren't at all like they used to be, in intensity. And most of the time, I knew I'd bring it on myself. But it's much easier to deal with when you know *you're* doing it than if it's something "out there." So the panic attacks certainly weren't as severe as before. And then I would start getting them right before my period, sort of in clusters. I'd also be a little blue just before my period, a little dizzy. I'd cry easily or I'd fly off the handle for the least little thing.

When I went to my gynecologist, I showed him this PASS course. I showed him the diet and everything, and told him what I was doing. He said, "Keep on with that diet." He explained that it takes a longer time when you're doing something nutritionally. It's not like when you take a pill and it's designed to clear everything up right away. But when you're doing things nutritionally, he said, it may take a matter of months. So I knew it was a process and that it took time to get over it.

How is it now? This month, I didn't even know my period was coming—until I looked at the calendar! I'm sure it's due to the diet and the exercise. Because I remember that when I was in high school and we had exercise in gym, I never had cramps or any of those other symptoms. But after the children were born, I became more sedentary. I wasn't getting the exercise I used to get. And then you're so busy with the children, you pop anything in your mouth for lunch—or you even skip lunch altogether. I remember having ice cream or things like that for lunch, just to get a quick lift. Now, of course, I watch what I eat and I exercise regularly, so that's what I think made the difference.

After being on the program a while, I began to notice differences about me. And my husband noticed it, too. Like I used to dread getting up in the morning. When the alarm would go off, I'd feel sick. I used to say, "Oh, no . . . ! Another day . . . ! I'm going to die today, for sure . . . !" It's nothing like that now. When I get up now, I feel *great*! I don't feel like I'm schlepping around the house. I get up, I take my shower, make my breakfast, get the kids ready—and we go out. I'm living a *normal* life!

What can I do now that I wasn't able to do before? I couldn't go out by myself before. And if I did go out with somebody—let's say, we were in a department store—if they moved away from me, even just to check something out at the next counter, I would panic immediately. Now, last week, for example, I went to Macy's alone. I bought some crystal and I also bought myself a hat for a wedding I'm going to on Saturday (I'm a "hat freak"; I love hats). I just went and did it—no problem! Now, I could *never* do that before.

I also couldn't be left alone. When I was alone in the house—and, technically, I really wasn't alone—I had my two small children, my cats and my dog!—but I would break out into a sweat. I'd start "what-iffing." I'd think, "Now, what if I have an attack and I pass out here on the floor . . . ?" Or: "What if this is really the Big One?" Now, it's almost a blessing to be all alone in the house when the kids aren't here.

Pete's Story

I'm a manager and, before I joined the PASS program, I'd work anywhere from seventy to eighty hours a week—sometimes more, even up to one hundred hours a week! In addition to my long hours, there was an awful lot of pressure on the job. Most of the time, I'd have to work under time deadlines. The hardest thing was working without adequately trained people—and they were hard to get. I live in an area where the unemployment rate is very, very low—less than three percent. In fact, we've had to bus people in from other areas to come and work in Rhode Island. So, without proper help, my job was that much more difficult.

My diet was pretty awful, too—mostly junk food. I would often skip breakfast altogether. And sometimes I didn't have a chance to eat at all until probably 6 o'clock at night. So I went without eating a meal, from dinner the night before. Many times, I'd just have snacks—potato chips, soda, things like that. If I had lunch, it usually consisted of sandwiches or a roll or white bread, with chicken or roast beef, and I'd wash it down with ginger ale or Hi-C.

But I've completely changed all that now. I eat a good breakfast. I eat all my meals—and I have decent meals. I stopped having junk food. I got myself on a well-balanced diet.

I've also cut down on my work load a lot. I requested and finally got another assistant. And this time they gave me qualified people. Before, I had basically new people who weren't as familiar with the job. Right now, I'm working no more than fifty hours a week. My work load is way down—almost cut in half, compared with what it was before.

When I joined PASS, I was very nervous—and not only at work. I couldn't go to a restaurant. I wasn't able to go shopping. I just avoided most situations. But my goal was to live a normal life; to be able to go out to a restaurant now and then and attend meetings and go shopping.

And now I can do all that. I can just about go anywhere and do anything. I don't get panic attacks or anything like that anymore. I can go to restaurants. In fact, just yesterday, we went to a restaurant and it was very nice. I enjoyed myself (and, of course, I ordered the right foods). In previous times, whenever I had to handle something personal, some crisis that was very stressful, I'd find it very difficult to deal with. Last week, there was a death in the family; my wife's father passed away. My wife was the oldest daughter, so there were many things we had to do. I did everything I had to, and my wife was surprised that I was able to handle the crisis and all that stress so well, without any adverse effects whatsoever. I see now that when your diet is better and when you're in better physical shape, you're able to handle much more stress.

If you're new to the program, my one word of advice is to definitely keep an open mind about this. Don't go into the program thinking this isn't going to work. Or how can changing the diet and things like that help you or have such a calming effect or cure you—because you think it's so bad, the panic attacks are so intense. But this program definitely *can* help. It's changed the course of my life considerably. I can pretty much do anything I want to now, without the fear of having a panic attack hanging over my head.

Phyllis' Story

I've had panic attacks since childhood, since I was about sixteen. They seemed to come out of nowhere. I remember the first time it happened: My heart suddenly started beating very fast and I felt like I couldn't breathe. The next time it happened, I was in school, and it was so bad, I had to go home. And then, when it happened after that, my parents took me to a hospital. The doctors examined me thoroughly and said it was "just nerves." I used to have air-hunger all the time—I'd gasp for air and I'd start to hyperventilate. And it used to bother me. I'd keep asking myself, "Why do I have to breathe like this??"

After I finished high school, I went to college. But, for a number of reasons—not only because of the panic attacks—I dropped out of school and got a job. I worked at a few jobs. Then I got a job as a waitress right across the street from where I live. I took the job because I figured, in case I get a panic attack, I can just run right home. Anyhow, I worked there for four years. But the panic attacks were getting progressively worse. They were always bad, but it was during the past three years that I could say the fear was just taking control of my life.

That's when I started seeing a psychologist. I wasn't in treatment long—only a couple of months. But there was no improvement. In fact, I was getting worse because I was constantly thinking about the panic attacks. The psychologist used to have me write down all my thoughts and feelings in a little book that I used to carry around with me everywhere I went. But that only made me focus even more on my problem. So that didn't work at all.

While I was still seeing my psychologist, I happened to read an article in the Sunday *News* about fear—and at the end of the article, they listed places where you can get help. That's where I first learned about the PASS program.

Changing my attitude has helped me the most. The turning point, as far as taking that big step forward, came for me when I was talking one night to Cindy, my counselor. She said I really had to start getting myself occupied and to stop worrying about how the other people on the program were coming along. Because at that point I knew all of my teammates were doing a lot better. And it bothered me that out of the four of us, I was the one who was in pretty bad shape. That conversation with my counselor was the turning point for me, because it was then that I decided that I wasn't going to worry about anybody else and how they were progressing. Not that I didn't care; but I wasn't going to worry anymore that they were coming along faster than I was. I decided to stop comparing myself to them. And I didn't care if it took me a year, two years—I would recover in my own time.

And that was when I started going to church more often. One night, I was outside near the church, talking to a girl I had just met. I was asking her all kinds of questions about the church, its beliefs, etc. Then this man joined us, and I told him about the panic attacks. And what this man said made such an impression on me! He said, "God didn't create you with a spirit of fear." He showed me the Bible, where Jesus says: "Peace I leave with you. Let not your heart be troubled, neither let it be afraid." I started to cry because, at that point, I really started to believe that what he was saying was true. I thought that no matter how long it would take for me to get better, I knew that this was the way I would do it. I would put my life in God's Hands and allow Him to lead me.

Now, when I do all those things I used to be afraid of doing, I have faith that God is with me. And *I am able to do those things.* I am working now. I am going out. I'm driving. I'm just doing everything. And I don't get panic attacks anymore. Once in a while, I might feel those little feelings come up, but I put my mind back on God—and the fear just goes away!

If I could give just one bit of advice to someone suffering from panic attacks, I would say this: You have to change your attitude. You have to believe in something. In my case, it's God.

Regina's Story

When I first joined the PASS program, I was very incapacitated by agoraphobia. I had suffered with this for many, many years. I was sixty-two when I joined the program. Although I was able to ride in a car, I could not stay in a store for more than fifteen minutes. Beyond that time, it was impossible. I had been in therapy with a psychiatrist, but there was no improvement.

Then, one day I saw an ad for PASS in *TV Guide*. I joined the program—and I never believed I'd get this far, but I did. I remember the first time I did something daring—and this was after I had been on the program for three months. (It was my biggest adventure in eighteen years!)

I have my hair done every week. My hairdresser, a lovely young woman, used to come to my house. One day, she told me she was getting married—and I received an invitation in the mail. The wedding was in September; I had started the program in June. But I was making such good progress with the program that I decided to go. I even went to a store (one of my "assignments") to buy a wedding present. When my daughter saw it, she offered to take it to the wedding, but I said, "Oh, no, you won't—I'm taking it myself." At first, she thought she heard wrong. She asked me, "Do you think you can?" I said, "I *know* I can!"

On the day of the wedding, as I was getting dressed, I was very nervous (the bride wasn't the only one!). But my faith in the program and the knowledge that I could do it helped me through. I sat—not in the back of the church, but right in the middle! The altar was beautifully decorated with flowers; it was a lovely ceremony.

The next step was the reception. I had come this far, and I knew I could stay. I sat down with a roomful of people (there were about one hundred guests) and enjoyed a delicious turkey dinner (of course, I didn't touch the dessert!). After they cut the cake, the dancing began— and I danced a few times (my husband isn't much for dancing). The bride was so happy to see me at her wedding. She asked jokingly, "Does this mean I'm fired?" And I told her proudly that from now on, she could expect me to be coming to *her* at the beauty parlor every week! I was very happy when I got home because I knew I had done something far beyond my dreams.

What else do I do now that I wasn't able to do before? Well, I'm back at church. I used to be a regular church member years ago, but when I had agoraphobia, then of course I couldn't go. One day I just decided I'm able to go and I want to go, so I went, and I kept on going! I attend service regularly now, and I like it very much. It brings me great satisfaction.

This summer, I've been going some weekends to visit my daughter. She has a camper in a trailer park and it's a two-hour drive from my house. I can go to the stores now—and to big shopping malls. Like I went to a mall last week with 88 stores in it and it didn't bother me at all. I was there over two hours. Sometimes when I'd go to a store, my husband would go away for a while for something and I'd be by myself, shopping. I can do it now; it doesn't bother me. But I could never be in a store alone before. Even with my husband there, I couldn't stay longer than fifteen minutes.

I've been to Canada recently to visit my sister. We went shopping there all day, and it didn't bother me. Traveling doesn't bother me at all now. I can travel anywhere and I can go to restaurants, which I certainly wasn't able to do before. I haven't had a panic attack in a long time, not in ages and ages! And I never thought I'd be doing the things I'm doing now!

Rita's Story

The panic attacks started with me when I was in high school. I was seventeen at the time, and that was a long time ago. I was bothered with that for a little while, but then the panic attacks left me, and they didn't occur again until years later.

It was never that I couldn't go out of the house or anything like that; it wasn't that severe. I didn't know what it was *at all.* I was just very nervous and panicky. I would just get nervous about things, but nothing happened to me, so I sort of "got out of it."

But then, as I said, years later, a couple of things happened that triggered these feelings again that I had almost forgotten about. It was just that different things were going on at once: I had been dating somebody for a pretty long time, and we broke up. Then, my mother had gotten sick—things like that. But this time—the second time I had it—I was more conscious of what was happening. I knew I wasn't "different." I realized these feelings were being triggered by a lot of the stuff that was going on in my life.

It wasn't that I ever *couldn't* really do anything. I mean, there were some things—like on weekend nights, when everybody was going out, I just didn't go out. Yet, I worked. I still went to school. But I didn't *enjoy* anything. It was just like a chore, trying to force myself to do these things. So that's when I decided to get help, and I was referred to PASS by my county mental health association.

The PASS program gave me some new tools to work with. Like the relaxation tape and learning how the body works and realizing that you're not the "only one" this is happening to. Dr. Weekes's book was also very helpful. My sister had the same problem with panic attacks, and she read this book, then she gave it to me. So I started reading it. To me, the most comforting thing was learning that the panic attacks never get any worse, that they can only go so far. And also, that you *do* have control over them.

I began to apply Dr. Weekes's four principles. I'd remember how she'd say, "Face, do not run away." That means just face it, just relax with it. Don't say, "Oh, my gosh, what's happening . . . ?!!" But sort of like don't think about it at all—like float past it, and stuff like that.

It was very helpful, too, when I learned about the home bases. It's funny, because that was how I would feel—like when I'd go someplace, I always used to feel safe in my car. It was like my home base, although I never called it that before. So there were many things I found useful. Like realizing that everybody gets edgy at times about different things. So if I'm edgy one day, I'd say to myself, "Well, don't put too much weight into it because it's only one day." A lot of pressure is off me now because I don't have to have things "perfect" all the time.

What I also found helpful was the advice I got from my counselor about the "worry hour"—to put all my worries into that one time-slot during the day. Because if you think about something all day long, it can get you crazy. This way, I knew I would worry about my problem a little later, whatever it was. So it definitely helped. It shortened my "worry time."

My biggest fear used to be going away places and staying overnight. Now, I can pretty much go anywhere. I own a boat, and it makes me feel good when I think that I'm able to go out on that boat and I'm able to handle things by myself. You know, being in a boat is quite different from being in a car. In a car, you can go out to make a phone call if you need help, or you can always pull over to the side of the road. But in a boat, you can't do that. My boat doesn't come equipped with a ship-to-shore radio. And even the driving is different; it's not like driving a car. There's a lot of maneuvering you have to do.

But I enjoy boating very much. I live on Long Island and I'm near the water. The couple of times I went boating before was with different guys that I went out with. And then one day, I just decided to buy a boat for myself. I took the course that the Coast Guard offers.

They tell you about all the things you have to know, like the waterways, how to read the markers, the channels, and the mechanical things on the boat. It was like a regular college semester, but in Adult Ed. There were a lot of married couples in my class, and a lot of older people; I was the only single girl in my class.

The weather is beginning to get warmer now and I'm trying to get my boat ready for sailing. This weekend, I was supposed to wax it, but I wasn't able to do it yet because it was raining. I really enjoy my involvement with the boat. I think it's a good idea to keep busy with something you really like. It keeps your mind off yourself.

Scott's Story

Since I put this program into effect, there have been enormous changes in my life. I'm able to work again. I go into stores. I can go up to the doctor's office. And there's a general feeling of well-being. Before, I felt like—"What's the use of going on like this?" At one point, things were so bad that I even contemplated suicide! I thought it was hopeless because I'd been that way for so long—thirteen years! (It started when I was about twenty-one—and I'm thirty-four now.) Finally, it got to the point that—three or four months before I started the PASS program—I was literally housebound!

The series of events that led to my becoming housebound and having thoughts of suicide were these: I lost my job because of the constant panic attacks. I had totally run out of money, and I decided I had to go out and get a job. I live in a small town and there aren't many jobs available. So I went to a large city nearby to look for work. But as I traveled, I found it harder and harder to get out of my car. (Instead of being housebound, I was becoming carbound!) It was so hard even to go to a gas station to get gas. But I had to do it, so I did. I'd wait around in my car until it got dark and not many people were there, and then I'd go up and get gas.

When I came back to my hometown, jobless, I moved in with my parents. (I'm single.) And I more or less stayed around the house, doing nothing and being miserable. Things just got worse and worse. And, after a while, I just became housebound. I couldn't go anywhere. Then, the bank called up that they were going to repossess my car for nonpayment. So that spurred me to get some help somewhere. A doctor came to the house and he prescribed Xanax, and that didn't do any good. He doubled the dosage, but it still didn't do any good. Finally, he gave me massive doses of Librium twenty-five milligrams three times a day. With that, I was able to go to the doctor's office regularly, but that was about it.

Just by chance, I picked up a magazine and saw an article about panic attacks—and they mentioned PASS. I joined immediately. At that point, I was willing to do anything at all that might help me. I loved sugar, sweets, chocolate and pop—things like that—but I just dropped them. I think if my counselor had told me to cut off my left arm to get better, I would have done it. I wanted to change so badly, I would have done anything!

At about this time, I met a man who worked at the bank (the one that was going to repossess my car), and who later became my good friend. He took me aside and asked me what exactly was the problem. I leveled with him; I told him about the panic attacks. He told me he understood perfectly because a while back, he himself had suffered from panic attacks. Looking at him, so self-assured, so confident, and a bank officer, I suddenly felt that I, too, could regain my confidence and self-esteem. This man recommended that I read certain books, like Wayne Dyer's book, *Pulling Your Own Strings*—which I did. (It's an excellent book and I reread it all the time.)

From what this man said, and from the books I've read since, I developed a new attitude that I call "aggressive friendliness." I simply radiate, all around me, friendliness combined with enthusiasm. And believe me, it really works! Whenever I'd feel intimidated by someone, I would just walk up to him, hold out my handshake, and give that person an enthusiastic greeting. An amazing thing would happen: I would no longer feel intimidated by that person! For example, there was this man I knew in my town, and he always used to give me problems. So, one day, I spotted him in the street. I pulled my car up to the curb, parked, and got out of my car. I called his name, walked over, put my hand on his shoulder and said, "How are you?" in a loud, friendly voice. And as I shook his hand, I could feel *him* shaking!

Another attitude I adopted is "Who the hell cares?" I'd walk into a store—and if I'd start to have a panic attack, big deal! I didn't care. If people noticed and got a kick out of it—well, that was *their* problem, not mine. So the panic attacks were cured almost overnight, so to speak.

When I was younger, I used to drink like mad to cover up my nervousness. I used to feel better when I was "loaded." So I gradually became a heavy drinker—and I did this for many years. But now I stopped drinking altogether; I don't do this anymore. How did I stop? After I started looking for a job and couldn't find any and I had to move in with my parents, I couldn't drink anymore. I couldn't get "loaded" in front of them—and I wasn't able to go to a bar. So I was, in a way, forced to stop. I actually had withdrawal symptoms. But, in a way, it was good it happened—now I don't need a drink to make me feel good. There are far better ways—like good food, exercise and relaxation.

Sharon's Story

I've been feeling fine. I've been eating well since I've been on the PASS program, but I'm especially careful with my diet now because I'm expecting twins in two more months!

Now that I'm home, I have more time to prepare better foods. When I was working, I'd have to get up early and we'd get home kind of late, so it was a lot harder getting good meals together. But now that I'm home, I can spend more time in the kitchen.

I had a thyroid problem at one time, and that, I believe, contributed a lot to my having panic attacks. But I don't have a thyroid problem anymore—not since they treated this condition with radioactive iodine.

I used to worry a lot about my health. I'd be thinking about illnesses and disaster all the time. I used to feel panicky over long periods of time. I found it difficult to go to work, and I had a problem sleeping. I used to have feelings of unreality. I couldn't go places without fearing I'd get a panic attack there.

Thank God I don't think that anymore! How did I change? I think I learned just to ignore those panicky feelings. What helped me most was just realizing that other people have these problems, too, and that it really wasn't anything. I found that when you turn your attention away from yourself, that those feelings really go away. In fact, I heard on the radio—they had this psychologist on, I think it was Dr. David Viscott. Anyhow, this woman called and she said she had these feelings of panic and she described it. She was afraid of dying. And he said, "Look, you're afraid of dying. But you're only going to die once—and it's not your time to die now." That's all it is. And that's how I've been looking at it, too. So these feelings don't bother me much, anymore.

I found out that in many situations, you have to just *do* the thing you're afraid of, and the fear goes away. Often, the anticipation is a lot worse than what actually happens. For instance: I used to be frightened about any kind of public speaking. But then, at work, I was promoted to a position where this was mainly my job—to speak before people. I wanted this promotion—and yet I didn't want it, because I had to hold meetings, and so on.

But I *did* get the promotion. And right off the bat, they told me I had to instruct a class of about thirty people, whom I didn't even know! These were trainees—new people who were hired. (I worked for a federal agency and they would hire a lot of people at once; there was a high turnover in this particular job.) They told me I had to do it. I had no choice. I wasn't about to quit my job.

Well, for several days before, I felt terrible. I just

couldn't help thinking about it. I was afraid. What if something happens to me in front of these people? On my first day on the new job, I got up there and I "shook." But to me, I sounded a lot worse than I must have come off. Because afterward, people were saying to me, "You were really very helpful"; "You were the best instructor I ever had"; and "We really understand what you were talking about." So, after one or two times, it became so easy. After a while, speaking before a group became so second nature to me; I looked forward to it!

Instead of thinking so much about myself and what other people were thinking about me, I started to think: Look, what's the difference—and if they don't like me, who cares?? I also put myself in the other position, like I'm in the audience, listening to a lecture. I remembered how I felt, listening to a speech and thinking how the other person up there came off sounding so good. Then, I'd find out afterward how nervous they were. And I couldn't imagine why, they sounded so confident and secure. And I didn't think any less of them for being nervous. I didn't ridicule them. Nobody sat there and laughed. So when I was on the other side, speaking, I imagined people were thinking of me the same way.

It's the same with panicky feelings. You can say to yourself, it's really nothing and you play it down and it goes away. I don't believe in looking into everything that you do and making too much out of it. I'm not doing that anymore.

Tracy's Story

I had a problem with recurrent panic attacks for the last ten years. My dream was to be free of the panic attacks and be able to enjoy more of my life.

I joined the PASS program because I read an article in my local newspaper about how a woman was helped through this program. When I first began the program, I found that it involved a great deal of eating—very much more than I was accustomed to. The decaffeinated coffee in the morning disturbed me because I felt I couldn't "get going" without that little bit of caffeine in the morning. But I soon got used to doing without it. Also, the vitamins and amounts of food—I just wasn't used to eating a lot. But my counselor helped me out with the food plan. I stopped smoking, too, as a result of this program, and the interesting thing about it is my weight stayed the same! My weight is absolutely normal. The reason it remained the same was because I compensated for the extra food by doing more exercise, more walking. Now I like the eating and exercise habits I acquired. To this day, I find I'm putting something in my mouth every three or three and a half hours. Before, I could go from breakfast or even skip breakfast altogether and not eat until, say, one in the afternoon. Now, I go munching along with my snacks. I feel better when I'm doing this. I don't know if it's psychological or not, but I just do feel better.

What things can I do now that I wasn't able to before? I can food-shop alone. I can go into any shopping mall by myself. I can get into my car and drive wherever I want to go. I feel free! Those were the things I couldn't do before. Of course, I worked even before I took this course. But my life is so much better now—it's freer and easier. Before the program, every time I stepped out the door, I would ask myself, "Will I be all right? How will I feel?" Now, I go out the door and say "I'm fine!" And I get in the car and I'm involved in where I'm going and what I'm doing. If I'm at a mall—and many times this goes through my mind—I remember the panic attacks. But I just slow down, do the breathing exercises and I get involved in what I'm looking at. I'd stop to check a rack out, check sizes, and so on. It passes, and I continue. Many times, while food-shopping, before the program, I'd buy six things—and leave them in the store and run out. Or I'd go to a place and we'd get there part-way— and we'd have to turn back home. So those are the things that are not anymore, thanks to the program.

I must tell you about this. A short while after I began

the program, we had a very big crisis—my husband suffered a heart attack. I was literally forced to drive on the highway, by myself, in order to get to the hospital to see him. But I put to use all the methods I learned from the program. I thought that was quite an achievement, being able to do that. When my husband was finally out of the hospital and recovering, his doctor told us he wants him to exercise, to walk. He suggested that he walk in the mall because it has controlled temperature there. Well, that was so traumatic for me. When the doctor said this is what he had to do, I thought I'd die. I said to myself, "I can't do this—malls—forget about it!" But then I had a big talk with myself. I said, "Look. You're eating correctly now; you're exercising, you're doing the relaxation. You're going to try this—because *he needs you!*" And, of course, my husband was nervous, too, because this was only three weeks after it happened, and he was not quite himself yet. But being I knew he needed me now, I went to the mall. We walked past three or four stores, and I looked at him and I smiled and I said, "This is fun—and I can do it." When you go shopping in a mall, you don't have to go—I mean, you really don't have to. But I had to go—because of him. If I couldn't go, he wouldn't have been able to go. So this program came along just at the right time. I put it all to use, all the information I got.

My husband's doctor told him to walk a half-mile, then one mile; now, we walk three miles a day. My husband is now on pretty much the same foods I'm eating, so that makes it a lot easier for me. He's got a stressful job, which he doesn't allow to get to him anymore. So we do these things together. We eat the same kinds of food and we exercise, we walk together. I feel it's such a small price to pay for what we've gained—what he gained and what I gained. These are the good things that have developed.

I feel now that I'm ready and that I really want to pass on this help. I want to help others as I've been helped. So I'm in training now to be a counselor for PASS. The counselor I had was so terrific and so sincere—I admire her very much. I used to think, "If I ever get to be as well as she is, I want to do this, too." Well, now I'm at that point.

Vivian's Story

Panic attacks have been a part of my life for the past five or six years, although the last couple of years were bad. But now, I just feel so good. I just feel like I'm a full person again. I didn't feel like I was an entire person at one time. My relationship with my husband is much better now because we go and we do; I was afraid to go anywhere before. Now, he yells at me, Can't we stay home? I say no. Before, he'd want me to go out, but I wouldn't go. I couldn't go to a restaurant—I was afraid I'd have a panic attack. I would avoid a lot of situations. I became good at making up excuses: something always "hurt" me. But now, come a Saturday night or a Sunday, and I say to my husband, c'mon, let's go, let's get out of here. And now my husband sometimes says, aw, not now, let's go later.

Like: Last week, my husband went to work and came home early. I didn't go to work that day. And—this would never have happened before—he looked at me and he said, "Do you want to go to Jersey?" Now, before, I would have made up every excuse possible not to go. But I just said, "All right." And I called up my sister and she said she was going to the beach club. Anyway, I put on my bathing suit and we got in the car. I couldn't believe it: We just got in the car and went! We went swimming at the club—it was beautiful there. And we came home. Now, I could never have done that before. Never in a million years. I never wanted to go to the beach—and I never wanted to go far. But this time, the next morning, I woke up my husband and said, "Let's go down to the beach again!"

So these are some of the things I'm doing now that I couldn't do before. I'm going away from the house—

even overnight. When I went away to Cherry Hill, New Jersey, the other weekend, that was the first time I've been there in years—and I loved it! I had such a good time, I couldn't believe it. I was there and nothing was bothering me. And the weekend before, we went to my other sister's house. It's like I can't wait to get up and go and get out of the house and do things. I feel great—so I'm just going.

How was it before I joined PASS? You know, it's hard to remember, I'm so far from it now! I used to be afraid to go out of the house before. I was afraid that if I had to run back home if I panicked, I wouldn't make it back. I had to always be within a certain distance, a safe distance. And I had to feel I was comfortable where I was going. So that, to me, was the best feeling—that I really went away and I didn't think of anything. And when I got home, I wanted to go back, so that's really great. I haven't had that feeling in years!

But back then, I couldn't do many things—like I couldn't go into an elevator alone. And even with somebody, I wasn't crazy about it. I used to get a panic attack every time I had to leave my house. I used to get random panic attacks, too—I'd be in a store, it would happen. I'd be driving, it would happen. For no reason, it would happen. Like I would just be sitting someplace, and I'd have one. Truthfully, my whole life then was just one big panic. I felt that no matter what I did, I'd get a panic attack. I couldn't work. And now I'm working full-time, every day, in my own business. I never even *thought* I could ever do what I'm doing. It's like my whole life is different. I just feel free. I don't feel that something is holding me back. I want to go and I just go. I mean, there are times that I still think about it—after all, it was in my life for so long—but I don't let it stop me.

Yvonne's Story

Till I was twenty, I was always a kind of "panicky type" person, but it never really bothered me. I didn't have panic attacks, but I had a tendency to get real panicky if I knew I was going to be away from home for a couple of nights without my mother. That used to make me real nervous. I just knew I didn't like it and therefore I avoided going away from home for a couple of days. Things got a little better when I was in my late teens. Then, I got married. I was married four years when I decided I wanted to have a baby. That's about the time it all really started—the panic attacks.

You see, I began dieting strenuously before I got pregnant. I wasn't too much overweight, but I felt like I needed to lose a lot of weight. I knew I would gain a lot during pregnancy and I didn't want to wind up looking like a blimp. My method of losing weight consisted of not eating all day long; I wouldn't eat a thing, except maybe drink two or three pots of decaffeinated coffee, along with a lot of diet pop. I would have one meal at six o'clock. So I would literally starve all day long and "pig out" on the one meal. I lost about twenty pounds during that period, but I messed up my metabolism to the point where I would gain weight if I had more than seven hundred calories a day!

Just about that time, my mother died in a tragic accident. She'd been my "strong person" all along, and that was, oh, so hard for all of us. I don't know how I ever got through it. My youngest brother was twelve years old at the time and I decided to take him to live with us (I was already married then). I didn't realize it at the time, but this was another great big stress for me, because I was working at the time, too. Then, my boss asked me if I would be interested in a promotion, which would entail going to school. I said yes, because it meant a big promotion. But, boy, did I have a lot to learn! I was under constant pressure at work, and I was going to school. My husband couldn't help me too much at home because he worked at odd shifts. So I wound up having *three* full-time jobs: going to work, going to school, and doing the housework! And the way I abused my body, so to speak, by not eating, by starving myself—all this set the stage for the panic attacks.

Well, I became pregnant and I had a little girl. (I only gained fifteen pounds during the entire pregnancy.) But my daughter was one of those "ornery" babies that cried all the time, although nothing was wrong with her. She just wasn't a happy baby. And that endless crying just drove me berserk! Because I knew that after six weeks, I would be going back to work. I finally did go back to work, and a few months after that, I had my first real major panic attack.

I was out to lunch with my friends at work. We were sitting in a restaurant, in a booth, and someone mentioned a mutual friend of ours. She told us she heard that that person had a nervous breakdown. Well, I just fell apart! My heart started pounding, I felt faint, a great sense of impending doom came over me, and so on. Naturally, I overreacted because I myself had begun to suspect that I was having a nervous breakdown because I was having such a hard time coping with everything.

But things were dramatically turned around for me after I joined PASS. I started eating the right things. I realized that exercise, combined with the right diet, was going to get me to lose weight if I needed to. I was reassured. I finally knew what was wrong with me. I think the phrase "nervous breakdown" scared me the most. I used to have all kinds of visions about what was going to happen to me: Would I go into a mental institution? What would happen to my baby? And so on. But then, I finally got the attitude of: "So what?" And I think that once I started turning all those what-ifs into "So what?" that it helped me tremendously. And I realized that things weren't that bad, anyhow. With this new attitude, I was also able to reduce some of the pressures in my life.

It was almost toward the end of the three-month counseling program that tragedy struck. By then, I had begun to feel a lot better. I could do a lot of things on my own; I could go pretty much anywhere I wanted to. Anyhow, I was going to work one day and I heard over the car radio that there was an accident at the company where I worked, a mining company. There was a fire in the mine and many miners were trapped underground! Nobody knew at the time whether they were alive or not. When I got to work, of course, nobody was working. The family members of the people who were trapped were already sitting in the offices, waiting for news. There was a tremendous rescue effort going on. So I was asked to man the phones, run the computer, and so on. The rescue efforts continued for days. One time, I was there for almost twenty-four hours. (I thought: Oh, this really is going to mess me up . . . I'm nervous as it is, and now I'm faced with death and grieving relatives and things like that.) I didn't know I could do it. But I did—I was able to help.

Where did I get my strength? I found that if my mind is not focused on me and what I'm experiencing and going through; if I'm able to focus on someone else or if I'm able to help other people—then that gives me the strength I need. It was a most valuable lesson to learn.

RECOMMENDED READING LIST

Diet

Everything You Always Wanted to Know About Nutrition by David Reuben, M.D. Avon Books, 1976.

Nutrition and Vitamin Therapy by Michael Lesser, M.D. Bantam Books, 1980.

The Save-Your-Life Diet High Fiber Cook Book by David Rueben, M.D. and Barbara Reuben, M.S. Ballantine Books, 1977.

Richard Simmons' Never Say Diet Cookbook by Richard Simmons. Warner Books, 1982.

The New Vegetarian Cookbook by Gary Null. Macmillan, 1980.

Diet for a Small Planet by Frances M. Lappe. Ballantine Books, 1975.

Nikki and David Goldbeck's American Whole Foods Cuisine (vegetarian recipes) New American Library, 1983.

Relaxation

The Relaxation Response by Herbert Benson, M.D. with Miriam Z. Klipper. Avon Books, 1975.

QR: The Quieting Reflex by Charles F. Stroebel, M.D. Berkley, 1983.

Exercise

Aerobicize, Ron Harris, Fireside, 1986.

Aerobics for Women by Mildred Cooper and Kenneth Cooper, M.D. Bantam Book, 1973.

Jane Fonda's Workout Book and *Jane Fonda's New Workout & Weight-Loss Program*. Simon & Schuster, 1984 and 1986.

Additudinal Change

Peace from Nervous Suffering by Claire Weekes. Bantam Books, 1978.

Psycho-Cybernetics: Self-fulfillment by Maxwell Maltz, M.D. Bantam Books, 1973.

Feeling Good: The New Mood Therapy by David D. Burns. New American Library; 1981.

New Guide to Rational Living by Dr. Albert Ellis and Dr. Robert A. Harper. Wilshire, 1975.

Dr. David Reuben's Mental First-Aid Manual by David Reuben, M.D. Macmillan, 1982.

Anxiety & Panic Attacks by Robert Handly with Pauline Neff. Rawson Association, 1985.

MAIL ORDER

Spencer-Hill, Inc.
Suite 131-B
3380 Sheridan Dr.
Amherst, NY 14226

1. These and other self-help books (including audio-cassettes and videotapes) are available through Spencer-Hill's Shop-By-Mail service. For mini-reviews and a price list, please send $1 to the above address.
2. To order the PASS-Group Relaxation Tape (mentioned on pages 66–67), please send $10.25, (check or M.O.) to the above address.

Have you been following this program? What were the results? What have you discovered about yourself? We would like to hear from you.

PASS-Group, Inc.
P.O. Box 1614
Williamsville, NY 14221
Tel: (716) 689-4399

Index